How They Prayed

Vol. 3—Missionaries & Revival

How They Prayed

Vol. 3—Missionaries & Revival

By Edwin & Lillian Harvey

UNITED STATES ADDRESS
Harvey Christian Publishers, Inc.
449 Hackett Pike, Richmond, KY 40475
Tel./Fax (423) 768-2297
E-mail: books@harveycp.com
http://www.harveycp.com

Copyright © 2021

All rights reserved. No part of this book may be reproduced or transmitted in any form or by any means, electronic or mechanical, including photocopying, recording, or by any information storage and retrieval system without written permission from the copyright owner, except for the inclusion of brief quotations in a review.

Printed in USA
First Edition 1963
This Edition 2021

ISBN: 978-1-932774-31-3

Cover Design by
Isaac Samuel
faithgrafikdesigns@gmail.com

Printed by
Lightning Source
La Vergne, TN 37086

Contents

Chapter

1. Henry Breeden 7
2. The 1857 Revival 15
3. The Welsh Revival 25
4. The Revival at Charlotte Chapel 35
5. Moody and his Intercessors 45
6. Finney and his Intercessors 55
7. Fraser of Lisuland 63
8. Missionaries in China 69
9. China Inland Mission 80
10. Missionaries in Japan 90
11. Missionaries in the Orient 100
12. Experiment in Revival 97
13. Missionaries in India 111
14. Missionaries in Africa 123
15. Until Sin was Uncovered 132
16. Revival in the Congo 136

FOREWORD

A series of articles, entitled "How They Prayed," appeared some years ago in our periodical, *The Message of Victory,* published in Great Britain for over forty years. These were prepared for our reading public by my husband and I, and have been gathered together and enlarged somewhat for this present publication. Our entire purpose is that the reader might be inspired to see the wondrous privileges and possibilities of prayer.

Over the years we have walked around our spiritual Zion, and have noted well her mighty bulwarks, towers, and palaces which, in effect, were men and women who had become convinced that in themselves lay no power or holiness of their own. Therefore they diligently sought unto the Lord, giving themselves to prayer and the ministry of the Word. Thus they became channels through which the unseen God could still make manifest His designs and purposes to their generation. Through their lips and pens poured forth hot words unctionized by the Holy Ghost until the truth of God stood stark and bold against the contrasting fogs and mists of worldly wisdom and materialism.

Then again, we have before us in the Bible pen portraits by the early disciples of our great Exemplar, Jesus Christ, Who did nothing of Himself but what He saw the Father do. He said nothing of Himself, but what He first heard the Father say. He did no deeds of His own initiating, without first ascertaining the Father's will. How completely He set aside His own personal will in order to glorify the Father alone!

If this book could but inspire a few men and women with a like passion to stand quietly in the Father's presence until they, too, could but speak His Words, then the time and effort and money would be well worth the expenditure. Never in the history of the world has there been an era of such great opportunity! May we give ourselves to prayer and the ministry of the Word!

Lillian G. Harvey, November, 1987

Chapter One

HENRY BREEDEN

"Shall I hide from Abraham that thing which I do?" (Gen. 18:17).
"But there is a God in heaven that revealeth secrets and maketh known . . . what shall be in the latter days" (Daniel 2:28).
"Surely the Lord God will do nothing, but he revealeth his secret unto his servants the prophets" (Amos 3:7).
"I thank thee, O Father, Lord of heaven and earth, that thou hast hid these things from the wise and prudent, and hast revealed them unto babes: even so, Father; for so it seemed good in thy sight" (Luke 10:21).
"God hath revealed them unto us by his Spirit: for the Spirit searcheth all things, yea, the deep things of God" (1 Cor. 2:10).

Henry Breeden lived in the Midlands of England at a time when other men of unusual spiritual stature, some of whom greatly influenced his life, were laboring for the Master. In the Nottingham area, these men were reaping large harvests from the seed which had been sown by earlier itinerants who had labored under great difficulties and sufferings. Their persistent efforts in sowing the life-giving Word, where formerly only deadness and formalism had prevailed, now produced a harvest ready for reaping.

Methodism may have had its critics, but there is one unmistakable factor which cannot be refuted—the godly men it brought to birth as a result of its travail. It is true that those who preach the Gospel leave their own impress upon their converts who resemble their spiritual parents whose ministry brought them into being.

It would seem from the verses quoted above that God is anxious to communicate His secrets to men who desire His kingdom's interests and His will above all else. God certainly, in a remarkable manner, conveyed to Henry Breeden His future plan for a revival which began in America in 1857. Let us see what it was that made Mr. Breeden a man whom God could entrust with one of His secrets.

"I came to a affixed resolve," he wrote, "that whatever else I was or was not, and whatever else I did or did not, I would by the grace of God become a man decidedly given up to prayer. And that resolve, I am thankful to be able to say, I have to a great extent been able to carry out. However other things have been attended to, the work of calling on the Lord has been my great and chief personal business. During the early part of life, however, though thoroughly given to this exercise, I had no settled arrangement with regard to the number of times for this duty to be attended to each day. But, a good number of years ago, I fixed it as a rule, that I would never pray less than a set number of times, chiefly in private, every day, God being my helper as long as I lived. And though since that resolution was formed, many years of hard labor have passed away, yet this duty has ever been attended to most carefully. But oh, how much to God I owe for His gracious help therein! And, thanks be to Him, I can look back on this with a happy degree of humble gratitude. Of a truth, I can say, I would far rather have it said that Henry Breeden was a man given much to mighty prayer, than that it should be gazetted that he was worth his unnumbered thousands of this world's wealth."

Shortly after becoming a local preacher, Mr. Breeden decided to become a schoolmaster. Finding that this occupation left him with much spare time, he earnestly employed himself in reading the biographies of godly men and women. This greatly affected his prayer life, as will be seen by the following remarks:

"Some time after giving myself in this way to reading, I was led to devote myself more fully to prayer. And so powerfully was I acted upon in this respect, that I made it a rule to pray at least every hour of the day. This, of course, could only be done during school hours in an ejaculatory way. That resolve, as to unceasing prayer, I was enabled to keep up for a considerable time. And the effects upon my heart and mind were very great. Indeed the good will be, I believe, as lasting as eternity! And on taking a calm review of the affair, I can most decidedly say, that if I had my life to come over again, I would give myself more to prayer than ever I have done."

And he came to realize that results were always proportionate to the energy exerted in that exercise of prayer: "With me it is a fixed rule that the spiritual good realized in nearly all cases, is exactly in proportion to the prayer made beforehand."

Men of prayer are invariably men of the Word, for reading God's Word is but the other side of prayer. We speak to God, but we also take time to deeply meditate on what He has to say to us through His Word. This Henry Breeden did with regularity as he states in his autobiography:

"It was a rule with me to begin in Genesis and read through to Revelation. And the first time I read the Scriptures entirely I was frequently weeping for joy. That Book has indeed been my pleasant companion, both by day and by night. As to how many times I have read the whole, from beginning to end, I never took any note, but certainly I must have done so once every year since my conversion.... I have striven to make God's Word my Sword. As a racer, to make its commands the Course on which I should run. As a traveler, to take its directions as my Map by day, and its lights as my Lamp by night. And, as a Christian mariner, to consult its warnings and soundings, as my Chart by which to steer. To search into its wondrous depths, to rely upon its precious promises, to look into its glorious plan of salvation, and to keep its beautiful commandments, I have ever striven to make my chief delight."

Later in his life, being stationed at a place for one month, he resolved to read over the entire Word of God in that short time, which he did, and leaves on record the blessing that such an overall reading of the Scriptures had upon his life.

Men who do not depend solely upon the Holy Spirit's assistance in the preaching of the Word are never so dependent upon God as to require much prayer in secret. The advice of a seasoned saint helped to impress Henry with the fact that only a Divine Agent could capture the citadel of man's heart and bring him in surrender to the God Whom he had offended:

"About this time I went to preach one Sabbath forenoon at Plungar, in the Grantham Circuit. There I was entertained at the house of Mr. Guy. He was a very holy, good man, who seemed to take much interest in young preachers. One thing took place during my conversation with him which made a most powerful impression upon me. While we were talking together he began to weep very profusely. Turning in his chair towards me, he said, with tears and great emphasis, three times: 'It is the power of God that saves souls, my lad. IT IS THE POWER OF GOD THAT SAVES SOULS, MY LAD. IT IS THE POWER OF GOD THAT SAVES SOULS, MY LAD.' That important sentiment the lad has never forgotten, and it has been a standard principle with him during the whole of his life. And he now confirms the statement. 'It is, it is, indeed the power of God, that saves souls!' . . .

"It now became a fixed principle with me, whenever I preached, to aim first at getting the people to feel their need; and then, to offer them the blessing they need. And this principle I have ever brought into use. When laboring to get sinners converted, or striving to get backsliders restored, or intent upon getting believers entirely sanctified, I have first attempted to get them, in each case, deeply convinced of their need. And I have had one rule which has been my guide in this respect. I have never, when in conversation with seekers, made an offer of salvation to them, unless I have had reason to believe that they did really and truly confess their need before Almighty God. This, as another rule, I have ever acted upon. In reviewing this affair, I am sure it was one great means of bringing about the success which Smith secured. And it has been one great secret in the production of any success which I have realized myself.

"I consider that true Gospel-preaching is properly an address to the human conscience. This made Mr. Smith say, on one occasion, when speaking of those men who were thought to be the better preachers of the day, 'I wish, Mr. Breeden, those great men would do a little more of the rough work, for then we should have more cases of conversion amongst us.'

"I resolved . . . that all my efforts to save souls should be in full reliance on the agency of God the Holy Ghost. And, therefore, that I would pray much beforehand for sinners to be saved; that I would pray very definitely for the salvation of certain individuals; that when I got very near to the Lord, I would always urge my plea with great particularity; that whenever God's great power came down upon me, I would plead with strong agonizing cries and supplications for the exertion of God's saving grace immediately."

All through his autobiography, *Striking Incidents of Saving Grace*, Henry Breeden constantly refers to seasons of intercessory prayer. Sometimes it is in nights of prayer; sometimes in seasons of public prayer in unison with other Christians; sometimes on a journey to another preaching appointment:

"About this time I preached at the noted town of Southwell, the place where I was born. I rose on the Sunday morning very early and spent a considerable time in prayer. God filled my soul in an extraordinary manner. In walking from Gunthorp to Southwell, I was engaged in prayer nearly the whole of the way. Many times I knelt down in the roads and by the roadsides for prayer, for it being early, the ways were clear of people. In the forenoon I preached in the open-air, at the silk mill. The power of God was very present; and, I believe, good was done. In the afternoon and evening I preached in the Wesleyan Chapel. That was, indeed, a day of much power from the Lord, like one of the days of Jesus upon earth!"

Around the Nottingham area, there were mighty giants of prayer in those days—David Stoner, William Bramwell, John Smith, and previously the John Nelsons, for there were two, and these all labored with mighty results. Favored indeed was young Henry Breeden with such associations both past and present. He tells what John Smith's friendship meant to him at this time:

"In the early part of this summer, Mr. Smith came to New Basford one week evening to preach for us by special arrangement. This was about the last time he preached for us before he left the Circuit. He was then to some extent restored from his great affliction, but not entirely well. A friend, therefore, said to him, 'I will lend you a horse to take you a part of the way home to Beeston, if Mr. Breeden will go with you to bring the animal back.' So I went with him.

"It was nearly midnight when we turned from the Derby Road down Beeston Lane, and the moon was then on the wane. As we were going silently along—he riding, and I walking—Smith began, in a most solemn manner, to pray aloud, and he prayed one of the most comprehensive dedicatory prayers that I ever heard or read. It reminded me very strongly of the prayer of Daniel, recorded in his ninth chapter; and of the Savior's sacerdotal prayer in the seventeenth of John; and also of St. Paul's great consecration prayer in the third of Ephesians.

"The occasion was most piercingly solemn. The hour was that of deep midnight. The atmosphere was exceeding calm and serene. The light of the moon was pale and flickering, and seemed to remind us of death. We were united, I believe, with as close an attachment as ever bound two men together in this world. I am of opinion that the attachment was not exceeded by the love of David towards Jonathan. Both seemed to have an impression that we should soon be separated from each other by the dire hand of death. And then the man had both the gift and grace of prayer to a large extent. And, added to these things, we both had the power of God working within us most mightily. His appeals to the Three-One Jehovah while he consecrated us, his appeals to the heavens to record it, his appeals to the earth and all things therein to remind us of it, bound both of us by the most profound and solemn ties to live and die for the salvation of immortal souls and for the glory of the eternal God. The good of that prayer has ever been upon me in a most extraordinary manner, and it has sometimes made me think of Elijah and Elisha, just before the fiery chariots and horsemen came down to take Elijah up to glory.

"But mainly and chiefly, my acquaintance with that great and Godlike man, the kind Rev. John Smith, was, of all other things, the great earthly advantage I received at Nottingham. For during the years of my residence there, I studied very closely, under his directions and instructions, the great principles of Religious Revivals and the great Bible methods of saving souls. And those helps have been of more value to me than thousands of gold and silver. And now, in the latter part of life, perhaps it is not too much for me to say, I got full well informed respecting God's great plan of saving souls—an attainment that has been to me of unspeakable value."

When this godly man was sixty he still sought to improve his life of prayer:

"November 22nd, 1864, was the time when I began to pray, by rule, a set and fixed number of times every day. I had been reading the life of the Rev. Andrew Lynn, of the Methodist New Connexion; and while reading it, I came to the conclusion that I would become methodical and exact as to my devotions. From the time I became a Methodist, I had been methodical in many things. But I had never set myself to observe method in regard to the number of times that I should pray each day. And I had found there was a great danger that the way of praying, at any time, might be *no* time. So I resolved that, come and go what would, 'set prayer should be attended to by me, at least, for my given number of times every day.' And I feel thankful to say now, after more than thirteen years, I have never failed for one single day to keep to my rule. It is true that in some cases, I cannot get into private for my devotions; but though I cannot retire, I can pray publicly or socially. Or, if traveling for a day, I can, and do pray mentally, and that sometimes very earnestly, while the carriages are whirling on their wheels. And in some cases I have prayed in that way, while traveling, and have received the most glorious answers and seen the best of results.

"And I bless God, my rule in regard to prayer still stands in good use. And I am as resolved as ever to keep in this way, to the duty. From the time of my conversion, I always prayed much—probably as much as I do now—but I did not, for many years, do it methodically. I feel grateful that I was ever led to fix on my rule, for it has had a very powerful and good effect on my heart, on my life, and also on my labors. The full amount of that good, can, I believe, only be known in eternity."

But perhaps the most remarkable incident mentioned in the life of this man of prayer is that time when God revealed His secrets of a coming revival to him during a concerted time of public prayer:

"At the Friday night prayer meeting we had a wonderful answer respecting the general Revival of Religion. I had been led out much in prayer for the outpouring of the Spirit upon whole nations, and indeed, upon the whole world. And the power to pray was, in this respect, **given** in a marked and high degree." (**We must pray in the Spirit, for He alone knows what is the mind of God**).

"And at last, when in an agony for the outpouring of the Spirit nationally, I had a distinct and deep answer given to me inwardly, which was nearly equal to having heard an audible voice, stating that in **twenty-eight years and three months,** God would pour out His Holy Spirit most abundantly and extensively. This I told to some of the praying friends as soon as the meeting was concluded. That period, however, I did not expect to live to see, for at that time I thought I should die a comparatively young man.

"Well, but time passed away, and various events took place, and I had nearly lost the thought of looking for an answer to those petitions, when to my great surprise, news came over to this country respecting the Fulton Street prayer meetings in America, and the extensive outpourings of the Holy Spirit. But how great was my amazement, when I began to calculate, to find that the great American Revival took place exactly twenty-eight years and three months after the time that I had received the above answer in New Basford Chapel.

"I am of the opinion that the Lord most surely made known what He intended in the future to do. And I think that was one of the secrets of the Lord that are given to those that fear Him. It was fully believed by us, at that time, that such a great national outpouring of the Holy Spirit would assuredly take place. And we were most fully persuaded then concerning things that were afar off, and we as fully embraced them."

Chapter Two

THE 1857 REVIVAL

In the preceding chapter we have seen the way in which God intimated to Henry Breeden that a revival would take place some twenty years later. This disclosure of one of God's secrets came while in a prayer-meeting in which the cry was for a general outpouring of the Spirit. It is not surprising to find that when the revival came, it was born and continued in prayer.

Account by Samuel Irenaeus Prime

From a book entitled *The Power of Prayer,* by Samuel Irenaeus Prime, we have the account of that movement of God in 1857 with eye witness records of how God moved upon hearts and communities. It was written just a year after those unusual gatherings for prayer which resulted in thousands of conversions. Some revivals have been marked by preaching with the unction of the Spirit upon them; others by singing, but this one seemed to be enveloped by prayer. It began in prayer; it continued in prayer:

"The pen of an angel might well be employed to record the wonderful works of God in the city of New York during the years 1857, 1858.... The autumn of 1857 was signalized by a sudden and fearful convulsion in the commercial world. That calamity was so speedily followed by the reports of revivals of religion and remarkable displays of divine grace, that it has been a widely-received opinion, that the two events stand related to one another, as cause and effect.

"In the day of adversity, men consider. When the hand of God is suddenly laid upon city and country, the sources of prosperity dried up, fortunes taking to themselves wings; houses, venerable for years, integrity, and success, tumbling into ruins; and names, never tarnished by suspicion, becoming less than nothing in general bankruptcy, it is natural to believe that men will look away from themselves, and say, 'Verily there is a God, Who reigns.' Never was a commercial crisis so inexplicable under the laws of trade. It was acknowledged to be a judgment. The justice of God was confessed in arresting men in recklessness, extravagance, and folly. Thousands were thrown out of business, and in their want of something else to do, assembled in meetings for prayer. But these meetings had been already established. The Spirit of God had been manifest in the midst of them.

"Before the commercial revulsion, the city and the country had been absorbed in the pursuit of pleasure and gain. Men were making haste to be rich and to enjoy those riches. *Recklessness of expenditure, extravagance in living, display in furniture, equipage, and dress had attained a height unexampled in the previous social history of our country, and utterly inconsistent with the simplicity and virtue of our fathers.*

"These signs of prosperity had filled the minds of good men with apprehension and alarm before the panic seized the heart of the world. Christians who had been kept free from the spirit of speculation and the mania for making money, had **trembled for the future of a people so absorbed in the material, as to be oblivious of the spiritual and eternal. These godly people had been gathering in meetings for prayer before the convulsion began.**"

***   ***   ***

How grateful we are that the false gospel of prosperity, wealth, health, and happiness had not gained a foothold or there would have been little hope for a genuine revival of the work of God upon the hearts of men. But let us now look at the instrument whom God used in a humble way to establish the first meeting for prayer in New York. The Rev. L. G. Bingham, who was among the first to witness these meetings, gives his account in Mr. Prime's history of this revival movement.

Account as given by Rev. L. G. Bingham

"In the upper lecture-room of the 'Old North Dutch Church,' in Fulton Street, New York, a **solitary** man was kneeling upon the floor, engaged in earnest, importunate prayer. He was a man who lived very much in the lives of others; lived almost wholly for others. He had no wife or children—but there were thousands with their husbands and fathers, without God and hope in the world; and these thousands were going to the gates of eternal death.

"He had surveyed all the lower wards of the city as a lay-missionary of the Old Church, and he longed to do something for their salvation. He knew he could do many things—he could take tracts in his hand, any and every day, and distribute them. He could preach the Gospel from door to door. All this he had done. To reach these perishing thousands, he needed a thousand lives. Could not something more effectual be done? So, day after day, and many times a day, this man was on his knees, and his constant prayer was 'Lord, what wilt thou have me to do?' The oftener he prays, the more earnest he becomes. He pleads with God to show him what to do, and how to do it.

"Though he prayed and believed, he had not the remotest idea of the methods of God's grace which were about to be employed. The more he prayed, however, the more confident he became that God would show him what He would have him do.

"Shall we describe this man? His age is not far from forty years. He is tall, well made, with a remarkably pleasant, benevolent face; affectionate in his disposition and manner, possessed of indomitable energy and perseverance, having good musical attainments; gifted in prayer and exhortation to a remarkable degree, modest in his demeanor, ardent in his piety, sound in his judgment; having good common sense, a thorough knowledge of human nature, and those traits of character that make him a welcome guest in any house. He is intelligent, and eminently fitted for the position which he has been called to occupy, which up to the present moment he has so worthily filled."

The man was Jeremiah Calvin Lanphier who was a native of New York State. He had come to New York City twenty years previously and was working in commerce. He was saved five years after coming to New York and went to the Tabernacle Church in 1842 where he stayed for eight or nine years. In the year of the revival, 1857, he joined the North Dutch Church, and undertook work as a lay missionary, July 1. No plan of work was laid out for him and he began laboring in the poor district of that large city. Rev. Bingham, who was with Lanphier from the beginning, had access to the man's personal diary and he shares the very first page with his readers.

Account as given by J. C. Lanphier

"July 1, 1857. 'Be not weary in well doing' (2 Thess. 3:13). 'I can do all things through Christ, which strengtheneth me' (Phil. 4:13). Read the fourth chapter of 2nd Timothy. Think I feel something of the responsibility of the work in which I have engaged. Felt a nearness to God in prayer, and my entire dependence on Him from Whom cometh all my strength.

"Going my rounds in the performance of my duty one day, as I was walking along the streets, the idea was suggested to my mind that an hour of prayer, from twelve to one o'clock, would be beneficial to business men, who usually in great numbers take that hour for rest and refreshment. The idea was to have singing, prayer, exhortation, relating of religious experience, as the case might be; that none be required to stay the whole hour, that all should come and go as their engagements should allow or require or their inclinations dictate.

"Arrangements were made, and at twelve o'clock noon, September 23, 1857, the door of the third story lecture-room was thrown open. At half-past twelve the step of a solitary individual was heard upon the stairs. Shortly after another, and another; then another, and last of all, another, until six made up the whole company! We had a good meeting. The Lord was with us to bless us."

No one was to speak or pray longer than five minutes so that those who could not stay long might be given an opportunity to take part. And so the first meeting that ushered in that mighty work of grace had very obscure beginnings, with only one man present for the first half hour and then five others arriving before the hour was finished.

The next meeting was a week later, September 30th, on a Wednesday. Twenty people were present at this prayer service at which time no formal schedule or procedure was maintained. The diary of Mr. Lanphier records the third prayer-meeting which took place on October 7th:

"Prepared for the prayer-meeting today, at noon. Called to invite a number of persons to be present. Spoke to men as I met them in the street, as my custom is, if I can get their attention. I prayed that the Lord would incline many to come to the place of prayer. Went to the meeting at noon. Present between thirty and forty. 'Bless the Lord! oh my soul, and all that is within me, bless His holy name.'"

Rev. Bingham Continues the Account

The Rev. Bingham again takes up his report: "The weekly prayer-meeting now was announced to become a daily business men's prayer service. A larger lecture-hall was soon procured. This meeting was of uncommon fervency in prayer, of deep humility and self-abasement, and great desire that God would glorify Himself in the outpouring of His Spirit upon them.

"The attendance has jumped to 100, and one month from the date of opening, Mr. Lanphier writes: 'Called on some of the editors of the religious papers to have them notice the interest that is daily manifested in our meetings.' But the revival had already begun before the press made any mention of it."

Early morning prayer-meetings began to spring up, and "the Broome-Street Church was one of the first to open a morning prayer-meeting. Other churches followed both in New York and Brooklyn, **without any preconcert or any knowledge of each other's movements.** Some time before any other was heard of and nearly simultaneously with the Fulton-Street meeting, if not before, there was instituted a daily morning prayer-meeting in the Plymouth Church, Brooklyn. In a quiet and unostentatious way, others were commenced, earlier or later. In the second month of the Fulton-Street meetings, several morning daily prayer-meetings were in existence.

"Denominational barriers were broken down during these prayer sessions. 'Never in any former revival,' said an eye-witness, 'since the days of the first Christians, was the Name of Christ so honored, never so often mentioned, never so precious to the believer.'

"It was not prayer–meetings in imitation of the Fulton-street meetings. *It was the desire to pray.* The same power that moved to prayer in Fulton Street, moved to prayer elsewhere. . . . Men did not doubt—could not doubt—that God was moving in answer to prayer.

"At the end of the fourth month, the Fulton Street prayer-meeting occupied the three lecture rooms in the consistory building and all were filled to their utmost capacity. So were all other places filled in the cities of New York, Brooklyn, Jersey City, Newark, and their vicinity. The three lecture-rooms at the Old Dutch Church had become filled to overflowing, one after the other, until no sitting-room or standing-room was left. Hundreds had to go away, unable even to get into the halls. How noticeable is one fact, and it must be noticed in order that we may see that 'the excellency of the power is of God.' There had been no eloquent preaching, no energetic and enthusiastic appeals; no attempt to rouse up religious interest. All had been still, solemn, and awful. The simple fact, the great fact was that people were moved to prayer. The people demanded a place to pray.

"So noiseless was this work of grace, that one portion of the community did not know what any other portion was doing in the matter. Who would have foreseen the connection of the meeting of six men for prayer in that upper room, in which was one Presbyterian, one Baptist, one Congregationalist, and one Reformed Dutch, with the events which were to follow? When was there ever such a meeting before? made up of such elements? met for such a purpose? at such an hour? and gathered up without the shadow of any human contrivance, as to any of the results which followed that haste with which God makes haste—'slowly.'

"Early in February, the old John Street Methodist Church, only one square removed, was thrown open for noon prayer-meetings by our Methodist brethren, and the whole body of the church was immediately filled every day, at noon, with business men, who would come and did come to pray. The galleries too were occupied chiefly by ladies.... It was estimated now two thousand persons attended upon these services daily.

"All over, the same spirit of prayer prevailed. No confidence was felt in the mere use of means. Indeed, in no former revival was there ever such **abnegation**, on the part of Christians, of themselves; such distrust of all mere human agencies and instruments, mentalities, and such a **looking away** from all human aid, and up to the 'heavenly hills,' whence all help must come.

"The first union prayer-meeting was not appointed to 'create a revival.' God had His own designs in view. The appointment of these meetings was to meet the demand of religious interest already existing, not to create the demand.... All these prayer-meetings have been the effects of a great first cause. God poured out the spirit of grace and supplication, and to His Name be all the glory.

"Even ships at sea were overtaken in mid-ocean—knowing nothing of what was transpiring upon the land—by unusual religious anxiety, and came into port bringing the strange news of a revival on board, and of the conversion of some of the men. Who can doubt but what the set time to favor Zion had come! The great feature of the revival everywhere was prayer—prayer by Christians united—prayer constant—each day sending up a cloud of prayer as a volume of incense before the throne of God—prayer that was divinely inspired and divinely answered. Such prayer has power—such prayer must always be heard—such prayer must prevail.

"The spirit of prayer was now moving to other large cities. In one meeting for prayer in Michigan a request was put in: 'A praying wife requests the prayers of this meeting for her unconverted husband, that he may be converted and be made a humble disciple of the Lord Jesus.' A stout, burly man rose saying, 'I am that man. I have a praying wife and this request must have been made for me.' As soon as he had quit speaking another man rose in the midst of sobs and tears, 'I am that man; I have a praying wife.... I want you to pray for me.' Three or four others rose requesting prayer.

"A father had three sons in distant and different parts of the country, all unconverted. He brought them to the meeting as the subject of prayer. They were prayed for as only those who believe can pray. What has been the consequence? Three letters have been received from these three sons, who have not communicated with each other, each giving an account of his own conversion."

Men of business came and prayed that they might be enabled to do business on Christian principles rather than according to the "laws of trade":

"A hardware merchant made an earnest address in the Fulton Street prayer-meeting, appealing to the brethren to set up a holy example in business, to have the same religion for 'down town' which they had for 'up town,' the same for the weekday that they have for the Sabbath—the same for the counting house as for the communion table. The address was four or five minutes in length, and was very effective. He was followed to his store by a well-known manufacturer with whom he had dealings for many years, and of whom he had bought largely.

"'You did not know,' said the manufacturer, 'that I was in the meeting and heard your remarks. But I was there. Now, sir, I have for the last five years been in the habit of charging you more for goods, than other purchasers. I want you to take your books, and charge back to me so much percent on every bill of goods you have had from me for the five years last past.'

"The same merchant told of another incident in his own business relations. 'I have received today,' he said, 'the payment of a debt of several hundred dollars, which has been due for twenty-eight years. The man who paid me today was just as able to pay me twenty-five years ago as today; but I had given it up and never expected to receive it, and I cannot account for its being paid now, but upon the supposition that the revival has reached the man's conscience, and he could not rest without paying that honest debt."

Account given by Rev. Dr. Murray

Thirty years previous to this revival, a prayer-meeting had been held in an old negro's humble dwelling in the near vicinity of Fulton Street. Rev. Dr. Murray, on his first visit from Elizabethtown, got up and related the amazing story of Aunt Betsy's prayer group. The account appeared in an old magazine:

"As I glanced upon the high brick stores in Ann Street, the memories of other days rushed in upon me. Where those brick stores now rise, upwards of thirty years ago there stood some wooden buildings, of very low pretensions. In an upper room of one of them, there dwelt an old colored woman, then widely known as Aunt Betsy, or Sarah—which, I now forget. She was very old, and very feeble, and remarkably pious. And some young men, mostly from the Presbyterian and Methodist churches, held a prayer-meeting in her room each Sabbath afternoon, as she was too infirm to attend on any of the public means of grace.

"While absorbed for a moment in these recollections, I was awakened from my reverie by a familiar voice in fervent exhortation. It was that of one who is now one of the princely merchants of New York, but in his youth he was one of the young men who met for prayer in the room of Aunt Betsy, and his wife was one of the little girls who, as the ravens did to Elijah, carried to her daily food!

"One of them rose to eminence as an accomplished writer and editor, and has served his country and the cause of Protestantism with distinction, as a Minister at a foreign Court.

"Another of them is an ex-Mayor of the city of New York, whose hand has never been withheld from any work of religion or philanthropy.

"Another of them is the honored partner of one of the largest publishing houses of the city of his residence.

"Another of them has risen to eminence as a merchant, and is a pillar in one of the most important congregations in the British Isles.

"Another is a well-known merchant of New York, who has a heart for every good work.

"Another is a useful minister in the Western States, whose labors have been eminently blessed in turning many to righteousness.

"I was myself among the youngest of the company, and when I was first invited to join the circle in the room of Aunt Betsy, was not a communicant of the Church."

These statements were made in the prayer-meeting, and after Dr. Murray had sat down, a man rose in another part of the room, his tremulous accents showing the feelings that were within him. "I have," said he, "recently visited the prison at Sing-Sing. As I went from cell to cell, I met with an old man who told me a very different story from that just narrated. He said that when young he was one of a company of young men who formed an infidel club, and who met once a week for talking infidelity, gambling, and drinking, not very far from the upper room of Aunt Betsy. And I was shocked as he told me of the end to which his companions came. 'One,' said he, 'died by his own hand; another by the hand of violence; some in the State Prison; some of *delirium tremens*; and, as far as I know, I am the only one of them surviving; and here I am in the garb, and daily at the work, of a felon.'"

***   ***   ***

And how did the revival affect the morals of the country? Vice and crime decreased. Even though the times were hard, and men, thrown out of work, could have plundered for bread, yet there was the staying power which prohibited an increase of burglaries. One man bent on murder and then suicide entered the place of prayer and found power to forgive, and the spirit of revenge was purged. Sharp business practices were forsaken, and doubtless could we have had the figures and statistics at hand we would see those dealing with the rate of drinking, immorality, etc., were lowered. There is no true revival existing today when teenage pregnancies are on the increase, when drug addiction is increasing, when alcoholism is devouring its victims and slaves, when the divorce rate is the worst in the history of the U.S.

Oh to see revival for the sake of our young children! When pregnancies among eleven-year-old girls are soaring, a revival would touch the children as it did in the 1857-8 revival. May God once again graciously visit His people with a spirit of prayer and intercession where our gimmicks and stage-acting are put away and we in contriteness and repentance appeal alone to God to work upon hearts, inclining them to prayer.

This revival of 1857-8 was the hand of God gathering people together for the sole purpose of prayer. "Where two or three are gathered together, there am I in the midst." Someone gathered those together with a desire for prayer. That Someone was in the midst to bless. There are people who wish to use prayer as a personal means of filling their church, of making a reputation, of going down in history as a great religious leader, but such are not "gathered together" by the Lord. "If two of you shall agree on earth as touching anything, it shall be done of my Father." That "agree" means harmonize. The subject upon their hearts has been prompted by the Spirit, which brings a harmony in asking that is bound to have an answer.

Chapter Three

THE WELSH REVIVAL

When proud man bends, the mountains flow down. This happened in a most decided manner in the life of that young Welsh miner, Evan Roberts, just previous to the outpouring of God upon the villages, towns, and cities of Wales during the 1904 revival. We can always trace the work of God to a praying figure, and there were praying people whose intercessions shaped the instrument used so mightily at that time.

Seth Joshua had prayed for four years for God to raise up an instrument, either from the plow or the mines, who would be used in the hands of the Almighty to bring the once religious principality of Wales back to its God. The spiritual condition was very low, and attendance at the house of God was poor. It was time for Him to work. Then there were praying groups, scattered here and there, whose sighs and cries were heard in Heaven. The instrument prayed for was being prepared by God for some years previous although unknown to those who were so deeply concerned.

When only a lad in his early teens, Evan had attended a prayer meeting. One night, the words of William Davies, the deacon, remained as a nail fixed in a sure place in the mind of the youth. "Remember," the deacon said, "to be faithful. What if the Spirit descended and you were absent? Remember Thomas! What a loss he had!" Evan shares the story of what followed this conversation:

"I said to myself: 'I will have the Spirit'; and through every kind of weather and in spite of all difficulties, I went to the meeting. Many times, on seeing other boys with the boats on the tide, I was tempted to turn back and join them. But, no, I said to myself: 'Remember your resolve,' and on I went. I went faithfully to the meetings for prayer throughout the ten or eleven years I prayed for a Revival. It was the Spirit that moved me thus to think."

I well remember how my husband and I stood on that little winding road which led out to Loughor, a mining village a few miles from Swansea. A local friend had taken us to see the blacksmith shop where Evan Roberts had worked for a time, and it seemed we partook of the spirit which still seemed to us to pervade that spot. Born in 1878 in the mountainous mining district of Wales, Evan also spent some of his working years down underneath those hills mining the coal, while the Lord was shaping His instrument to mine the souls of men.

Later, a call to preach produced a struggle in his heart. Finally he yielded, saying, "For me a grave or a pulpit." The preparatory school for ministers to which he went was presided over by a godly man who encouraged the students to seek for a deeper experience of grace. Even at this period, the young ministerial student was spending nights in prayer for revival.

Already the sound of a coming movement was in the air. Here and there were tokens of a future blessing. At a Keswick Convention held at Llandrindod in Wales in 1903, Evan Roberts heard the late F. B. Meyer speak. He, too, had likewise been praying for a revival for many years. The obedience of a young woman who rose up at this gathering and said, "I love Jesus Christ with all my heart," unleashed a small rivulet of grace which was but the forerunner to the floods which were to inundate Wales a year later.

When God sees a person bent upon being all for Himself, He will move Heaven and earth to bring that person into contact with the right individuals. Seth Joshua, an evangelist with the Forward movement of the Presbyterian Church, went to a place in Cardiganshire to hold special meetings. Some of the young students from the preparatory school were there, Evan among them. One of the hymns sung was "Bend Me Lower." The presence of God was again felt in a marked way. Evan Roberts was under the burden of prayer, and in this service he had a vision of God's condescending love to sinners.

The Spirit was saying to the young man, "You need to be bent." Speaking of this momentous time in his spiritual history, he records: "I felt some living energy or force coming into my bosom. It held my breath. My legs trembled terribly. This living energy increased as one after the other prayed until it nearly burst me.... My bosom was boiling and if I had not prayed I would have burst.

"What boiled in me was that verse: 'God commendeth His love.' I fell on my knees with my arms stretched out over the seat before me. The perspiration poured down my face, and my tears streamed so quickly I thought the blood came out.... I cried, 'Bend me, bend me!' I thought the blood was gushing forth."

Certain friends there approached him to wipe his face while he continued to call out: "O, Lord, bend me! Bend me!" The Lord answered that prayer and Roberts continues:

"After I was bent, a wave of peace came over me and the audience sang, 'I hear Thy welcome voice.' And as they sang I thought about the bending at the Judgment Day and I was filled with compassion for those that would have to bend on that day, and I wept. Henceforth the salvation of souls became the burden of my heart. From that time I was on fire with a desire to go through all Wales, and if it were possible, I was willing to pay God for the privilege of going."

Back at school, the young man felt a loneliness and isolation as he was eyed rather suspiciously by those who could not understand his recently acquired burden for others, and the overwhelming love of God which had been shed abroad in his heart by the Holy Ghost. He felt led to leave the school and return to his own village of Loughor to hold some services. Here he mentioned four requisites for revival:

1. Past sin had to be confessed.
2. Anything of a doubtful nature had to be put away.
3. Do whatever the Spirit of God prompts you to do. For, said he, it is better to offend men than to grieve the Spirit of God.
4. A personal confession of Christ as Savior.

Speaking of these services, he explained his procedure there. "At the beginning of the revival, the usual meetings held in Loughor were for one hour. I went there on the Monday night, began at 8:15, and went on for two hours. Every night, we went on with the meetings until I felt, and they all felt, that the work for that meeting was accomplished, every night working with the Holy Ghost, until the work for that particular meeting was done.

"In the fourth meeting the one thing emphasized was that they should confess Christ as their Savior. There was a lack of that—ten only confessed, and felt there was a stiffness to confess. I prayed on that one point. I determined to wait unto dawn before leaving the place, and prayed and prayed and prayed. After a time we had ten, not converts but church members, to make a confession in public. It was a declaration of their faith, not an acceptance of Christ. After some ten minutes there came the eleventh, and in less than half an hour there were twenty; and I felt that something had been done. They used the power they had. They had confessed Christ, and they all felt as if they had some great joy, and that opened them to receive. Each one must use what he has before he will get more. Perhaps in this case they did not like the public confessing, and others may not like it; but they must do it, like or not like, and then if they will obey, God will work upon their volition.

"In the seventh meeting, in the seventh hour, I was impressed to pray—not only to 'hope,' but to pray and believe that the Holy Ghost would come down and come THAT VERY MOMENT. THE FAITH WAS GIVEN.... There would be about one hundred present, and I was in the big pew, and there I sat and I prayed a definite prayer, then each one prayed it. Half through the congregation, there was a movement and somebody was crying under the gallery—one here, one there. Afterwards it transpired that there was more than one in the same pew upon whom God worked.

"The difficulty is to get meetings in which the work is accomplished. Workers go so far, then stop.... There is a beginning, and ending, and you must know when there is an end to God's purpose for that meeting, and work with God until it is done. There is too much trifling with God. There is a lack of cooperation with Him. They will 'pray,' but He will never come by prayer alone. The value of prayer lies in its answer."

Rapidly the fire of revival spread to other parts of Wales. Dr. F. B. Meyer and G. Campbell Morgan wished to see for themselves what was going on, so they visited the area in the early days of the movement. Outside the railway station at Cardiff they accosted a policeman, asking him where the revival was. Putting his hand on his heart and with face aglow he replied, "Gentlemen, it is here." So they had a favorable impression from their first contact.

F. B. Meyer's impressions of the man God was so mightily using in the salvation of souls have been left recorded. "F.B. Meyer saw one evening a young minister come into a crowded service. During the meeting he stood up and prayed for two of his unsaved friends who were scoffing in the gallery. One of them immediately arose and said, 'I am not scoffing. I am simply saying I am not an infidel but an agnostic. If God wants to save my soul I will give Him an opportunity. Let God do it.'

"This boast seemed to strike Evan Roberts so that he fell on his knees in a perfect agony of soul. It seemed as though his very heart would break beneath the weight of this man's sin.

"A friend of Dr. Meyer's who stood near him said, 'This is too dreadful! I cannot bear to hear this man groan so! I will start a tune to drown it!'

"Dr. Meyer, said, 'Whatever you do, don't do that. I want this thing to sink into my heart. I've preached to great masses of people without turning a hair; I want the throb of this man's anguish to touch my own soul.'

"Evan Roberts sobbed on and on and Meyer said, 'My God, let me learn that sob, that my soul may break while I preach the Gospel to men.'

"After about ten minutes Roberts arose and addressed the men in the gallery: 'Will you yield?' They said, 'Why should we?' Then he said to the people: 'Let us pray.' The air became heavy with sighs, tears, and groans. Everybody seemed to be carrying these two men upon their hearts, as if their hearts must break beneath the strain.

"Meyer declares that he never felt anything like it. He sprang to his feet; he felt as though he were choking. He said to his friend: 'We are in a very fight between Heaven and hell. Don't you see Heaven pulling this way and hell that? It seems as though one heard the beasts in the arena.'

"Soon one of the men yielded. The other went his way like the impenitent thief. If it took that to reach men in the great Welsh Revival, will it not take the same today?

"'O wall of the daughter of Zion, let tears run down like a river day and night: give thyself no rest. . . . Arise, cry out in the night: in the beginning of the watches pour out thine heart like water before the face of the Lord' (Lam. 2:18-19)."

Here are some of the impressions which Campbell Morgan shared with his congregation in Westminster: "In connection with the awakening there was no preaching, no order, no hymn books, no choirs, no organ, no collection, and finally, no advertising. Now, think of that for a moment again will you? Think of all our work. I am not saying these things are wrong. I simply want you to see what God is doing.

"There were the organs, but silent; the ministers, but among the people, rejoicing and prophesying with the rest, only there was no preaching. Yet the Welsh Revival is the revival of preaching to Wales. Everybody is preaching. No order, yet it moves from day to day, week to week, county to county, with matchless precision, with the order of an attacking force. No song books, but ah, me, I nearly wept tonight over the singing of our last hymn. When the Welsh sing they abandon themselves to their singing. We sing as though we thought it would not be respectable to be heard by the one next to us. No choir, did I say? It was all choir!

"And hymns! I stood and listened in wonder and amazement as the congregation sang hymn after hymn, without hymn books. Oh, don't you see it? The Sunday School is having its harvest now. The family altar is having its harvest now. The teaching of hymns and Bible among those Welsh hills and valleys is having its harvest now.

"There was no advertising. The whole thing advertised itself. You tell me the press advertised it. I tell you they did not begin advertising it until the thing caught fire and spread. And let me say to you, one of the most remarkable things is the attitude of the Welsh press. I came across instance after instance of men converted by reading the story of the revival in The Western Mail and the South Wales Daily News.

"In the name of God let us cease trying to find it! At least let us cease trying to trace it to any one man or convention. You cannot trace it. And yet I will trace it tonight. Whence has it come? All over

Wales—I am giving you roughly the result of the questioning of fifty or more persons at random in the week—a praying remnant has been agonizing before God about the state of this beloved land, and it is through prayer the answer of fire has come.

"You tell me that the revival originates with Evan Roberts. I tell you that Roberts is a product of the revival. You tell me that it began in an Endeavor meeting where a young girl bore testimony. I tell you that was the result of a revival breaking out everywhere.... It is a Divine visitation in which God—let me say this reverently—in which God is saying to us: 'See what I can do without the things you are depending on; see what I can do in answer to a praying people; see what I can do through the simplest, who are ready to fall in line, and depend wholly and absolutely upon Me.' Within five weeks twenty thousand have joined the churches.

"What effect is this work producing upon men? First of all, it is turning Christians everywhere into evangelists. There is nothing more remarkable about it than that, I think. People you never expected to see doing this kind of thing are becoming personal workers....

"The revival is characterized by the most remarkable confession of sin, confessions that must be costly. I heard some of them, men rising who have been members of the church, and officers of the church, confessing hidden sin in their heart, impurity committed and condoned, and seeking prayer for its putting away. The whole Welsh Revival is marvelously characterized by a confession of Jesus Christ, testimony to His power, to His goodness, to His beneficence, and testimony merging for evermore into outbursts of singing.

"Oh, brothers, sisters, Pray, Pray, Pray alone! Pray in secret! Pray together! And pray out of a sense of the world's sin and sorrow."

W. T. Stead wrote for London's Daily Chronicle: "There was absolutely nothing wild, violent, hysterical, unless it be hysterical for the laboring breast to heave with sobbing that cannot be repressed, and the throat to choke with emotion as a sense of the awful horror and shame of a wasted life suddenly bursts upon the soul. On all sides there was the solemn gladness of men and women upon whose eyes has dawned the splendor of a new day.

"Employers tell me that the quality of the work the miners are putting in has improved. Waste is less; men go to their daily toil with a new spirit of gladness in their labor. In the long, dim galleries of the mine, where once the hauliers swore at their ponies in Welshified English terms of blasphemy, there is now but to be heard the haunting melody of the revival music. The pit ponies, like the American mules, having been driven by oaths and curses since they first bore the yoke, are being retrained to do their work without the incentive of profanity.

"There is less drinking, less idleness, less gambling. Men record with almost incredulous amazement how one football player after another has forsworn cards and drink and the gladiatorial games, and is living a sober and godly life, putting his energy into the revival. . . .

"Two-thirds of the congregation were men and at least half were young men, stalwart young miners, who gave the meetings all the fervor and swing and enthusiasm of youth. . . . The last person to control the meeting in any way is Mr. Evan Roberts.

"People pray and sing, give testimony, exhort, as the Spirit moves them. As a study of the psychology of crowds, I have seen nothing like it. You feel that 1,000 or 1,500 persons before you have become merged into one myriad-headed but single-souled personality."

D. W. Lambert, in an article on the revival in Wales, said of the results: "While the revival was emotional (it was working on Celtic soil), it was also ethical. The Spirit of God did His own work of conviction as the standard of restitution was set up. A young man would return his prize medal or diploma because he had gained it unfairly. Long-standing debts were paid, and stolen goods returned. Prize fighters, drunkards, gamblers, and publicans, were savingly transformed. Magistrates had no cases to try and public houses were deserted. Prayer-meetings were held underground, and it is said that even the pit ponies felt the revival in the changed language and manner of their masters.

"Above all, this was a revival of prayer. It began in prayer and prayer was the keynote all through. In many meetings there was no preaching or speaking, just a great volume of prayer and praise going up to God."

The revival suddenly ceased in 1905 when many thought it could not be contained without spreading worldwide. Always when there is a work of God, Satan is unusually busy imitating the Spirit's work. My husband and I held meetings in the very area where the revival had had its greatest impact. The little chapel in which we ministered had been one of the first in which mighty grace had wrought miracles. We met those who had been subjects of the revival, and there was something marked about them. The prints of the hobnailed boots had left their impression on the old forms, and as we listened to their heavenly singing, we had to admit that if it was so wonderful when no revival was in session, what must it have been when God was moving upon thousands, touching the heart strings and loosing lips long sealed!

We listened to stories firsthand, related by men well on in years who had witnessed God's movements in the revival. We begged for some of these personal reminiscences to be written down for future generations to read, but the chief historian who could have done it was removed shortly afterwards by death.

What had caused the sudden withdrawal of the instrument Evan Roberts? One said that there was an evening when multitudes had gathered beneath the window of the building where Evan Roberts was staying chanting, "We want Evan Roberts. We want Evan Roberts." Finally he did appear on the balcony acknowledging the crowd's insistent demand. Some declare that Evan Roberts that night took glory for what God alone had done, and was never the same. This would require further verification.

The biographer of Mrs. Jessie Penn Lewis gives this short explanation: "Through the strain and suffering brought upon him during eight months of daily and continuous meetings in crowded, ill-ventilated chapels, one of the chief figures of the awakening in Wales completely broke down, and thus it came about that, by the invitation of Mr. and Mrs. Penn-Lewis, Mr. Evan Roberts went down to the country home near Leicester, where they were now living, for a time of rest and recuperation. His recovery, however, was slow and intermittent, lasting many months, and during the long period of convalescence, he began to open his mind to the hostess on many experiences of supernatural forces witnessed during the Revival. Since her own mighty enduement of power for service, Mrs. Penn-Lewis had learned the path of the Cross, and seen the dangers attendant upon souls who, having experienced such a breaking-through into the supernatural realm, do not know identification with Christ in His death as the place of safety from the wiles and assaults of the devil."

During his stay in this gracious home, he, together with his hostess, authored a book, *War on the Saints*, enlightening many Christians as to the subtle attacks of Satan upon the work of God and upon individual souls. He often strikes his heaviest blows at the saintliest of men and women. Satan is more active when God is active through His Holy Spirit. At the beginning of the original, unabridged edition of the above book there is this word: "As the key is to the lock, so is this book to the Christian." Upon reading it, one is aware that the authors were acquainted with Satanic wiles and wished to admonish others. Out of the greatest movement of God can come many subtle attacks of the evil one bent on discrediting the work of God. This book is doubtless a prize coming from one who, firsthand, fought most fierce conflicts with the prince of the power of the air.

Chapter Four

THE REVIVAL AT CHARLOTTE CHAPEL

God had for years been preparing the chief human instrument for what was to prove a most remarkable revival. This chosen vessel, Joseph Kemp, began life with few outward advantages. His father, a policeman, was drowned when the lad was but seven years old and a sense of responsibility toward the family of six brothers and sisters early devolved upon the child. Though the boy did not as yet know Christ as his Savior, he had an inner faith that, when food was scarce and bills were overdue, prayer to his heavenly Father would bring the needed supplies. And the many answers to his childish prayers laid the foundation for a prayer life which was remarkable.

Two years after his father's death, his mother also was taken from him, and he and his siblings were separated, living in different homes. Joseph, however, kept in touch with his sisters. God Who cares for the widow and the fatherless raised up a spiritual friend for the orphan boy. In that city of Hull in Yorkshire, England, Mr. J. Russell, who had also been orphaned when young, felt for the bereaved boy and took an interest in him. To this friend Joseph owed his deep reverence for the Word of God, for when he once had to leave Hull for a time to work in another town, he was sent a gift of a Bible, accompanied by a fatherly letter begging the lad to read the precious Volume. In the front of that Bible Mr. Russell had put that verse, "He that believeth not is condemned already." The word "already" was underscored, and this verse was deeply written on the boy's heart.

In one of his letters, Mr. Russell had given this short petition for the boy to pray: "Lord, take my heart, and give me Thy Holy Spirit."

But it was to an old weather-beaten Christian sailor that Joseph owed his entrance into the Kingdom of God. Sitting with him one day, the old man addressed the boy with a serious query as to when he would choose Christ, and Joseph, with determination, replied, "I will do so, now." On the way home he didn't feel any different, but he knew he had made a transaction and was now a child of God. He remembered the many warnings faithfully given by Mr. Russell. Now he no longer felt he was condemned for he had believed. He never again feared that word "condemned."

Another link in the program of preparation for this vessel of usefulness was his introduction into the neighborhood church, where the minister was the Rev. W. P. Mackay, author of *Grace and Truth*. This book helped bring salvation to Paget Wilkes and also to Bishop Hannington who was martyred for the faith. With such a man for his minister, Joseph's foundations for the future were being laid carefully and soundly.

Many and varied are the experiences of God's servants. But will it not be revealed in that great day that all profound workings of the Holy Spirit have been wrought through infilled instruments—the consecrated lives of those who have "kept nothing back" from Him Who gave His all for them? Scholars may wrangle. Theologians may analyze. But a work of the Spirit requires a Spirit-filled man. And at sixteen, Joseph Kemp was brought into a deeper experience through listening to a series of sermons conducted by the uncle of Graham Scroggie. Sitting in the gallery night after night, the youth became convinced that there was a wealth of riches to be had in Christ Jesus for the fully yielded believer.

Through one sermon, "Be Ye Separate," Joseph was convinced that he must yield his all to Christ now, reserving nothing for himself. A way of complete obedience loomed up before the seeker, and from his heart he vowed obedience to the Holy Spirit so as to be used by Him. Great joy resulted.

But it was to that man of God, Andrew Murray, that this now dedicated servant of God owed so much, for he it was who seared into his very soul the important place that prayer should take in the life of a Christian. Joseph tells of that memorable meeting when the speaker added a dimension to his life never to be forgotten: "In company with several of my fellow-students, I was attracted to the meeting by the announcement that the Rev. Andrew Murray of South Africa was to speak. The subject dealt with I do not remember. Whether the hall was crowded or not, I have not the remotest recollection. One thing and one only, stands out vividly in my memory as having taken place on that, to me, unforgettable night. It was the slim, solemn, and somewhat stern figure of Dr. Murray, when he stood before his audience as a man with a weight upon his soul. Erect and earnest, he shot his index finger into the air and cried, 'WANTED: MEN WHO CAN PRAY!'

"I have never forgotten it. The effect of it was overpowering. Its very appeal was a rebuke, and the memory of it haunts me as I write. I have listened to great preachers and not least among the number was Andrew Murray himself; but no preacher ever stirred my soul as did that appeal. I have revelled in the sound of mighty music, but none ever thrilled me as did that call to prayer. I have read every book on prayer which has fallen into my hands; and, with the solitary exception of Bounds on Prayer, nothing has touched my soul as that word of Murray's as it came crashing through the air in the Glasgow Convention.

"Here after over thirty years it has come to me again; and I can no more get rid of it than I can rid myself of my own shadow. Like John on Patmos, I hear a voice saying to me, 'Write,' and in obedience, my pen is active. I have thought, 'What would Andrew Murray say if he were with us today?' His call, I am certain, would not be less insistent; certainly, it is not less necessary, for of all things the Church needs to be called to in our day, it is prayer."

Joseph's biographer says of his life after this: "Now, as the message gripped his soul, he gave himself to prayer as never before; and with the Holy Spirit's guidance day by day his faith was strengthened. As he worked he prayed, and God came and filled his life. He was very practical, and soon got the secret of 'praying without ceasing.' He learned the sweetness of the abiding Christ through prayer, and prayer became a habit in his busy life. How precious was this experience. In the Monday night 'praise and prayer' meeting in Prospect Street Church, Hull, he had learned from W. P. Mackay the large place that praise should take in a Christian life; and he never forgot the lessons he received there. It took a tremendous place right through his life."

After a two year course at B.T.I. (Bible Training Institute), he graduated with a Diploma of Merit of the first grade. First he labored as an Evangelist in Ayrshire and then in turn served a pastorate in two Scottish Border Baptist congregations in Kelso and Hawick. At his induction, he was pleased to see his childhood friend, Mr. Russell, in the audience. At Kelso he became acquainted with the Binnie family and it was to their daughter, Winnie, that he was united in marriage before taking up his new duties at Hawick. Close budgeting of finance was vitally necessary, and he gave himself to prayer and to study, setting aside the mornings for this purpose. He was always deeply burdened when he saw young ministers trifling away the early part of the day.

Joseph Kemp had decided that New Testament methods would be adopted throughout his ministry. He preached with few notes, trusting to give the Holy Spirit more room in which to operate. Some thought their young pastor's methods were a bit drastic and too farfetched for the times, but he fearlessly adhered to his principles and advanced in grace and in fruitfulness.

An urgent call came to him from Charlotte Chapel. This was a test of consecration, for the congregation was small and the finance limited. Furthermore, he found the climate of Edinburgh did not agree with his health. But the secretary of Charlotte Chapel was insistent and sure that Joseph Kemp was God's instrument for their church. This secretary, Mr. Urquhart, was a man of prayer and vision. By the eyes of faith he foresaw the coming revival as a secret entrusted to him by the Holy Spirit.

"Look, Look! See the crowds," he exclaimed to his family as they wended their way one Sunday morning to the chapel. The street was empty and the children could not see with the natural eye what the eye of faith saw.

"Where father?" they asked. "Where are the crowds?" But Mr. Urquhart's vision gave him that inward witness of better things ahead for the straggling congregation who had almost lost heart.

The one seeming personal advantage in Joseph's new location was that here was the University where he could, perhaps, by dint of great economy of time, get his degree. His childhood education had been meager indeed, and though he had trained at the B.T.I., he longed for further acquirements in the educational field.

But Joseph Kemp soon saw that it must be a choice between more learning or the much-needed revival. He chose the latter, and instead of losing himself in studies, he began an intense private and public prayer campaign, arranging prayer-meetings whenever and wherever possible. Like Murray McCheyne, who at the height of revival in Dundee reported 39 weekly prayer-meetings, Mr. Kemp felt that they could not have too many of these "powerhouse" gatherings.

Mr. Kemp had been a sufferer from asthma and nasal catarrh, and the unfriendly climate of this Scottish city aggravated his condition considerably. His having spent the whole of Saturday night sleepless due to asthma would never deter this man of God from making the one mile walk to the Chapel in order to attend the 7 o'clock prayer-meeting. In fact, four times on the Sabbath he wended his way there, often in winter times wading through slush and wet, fulfilling an eight mile journey on foot each Sabbath day. He did not wish any leniency on his part to lessen the urgency in intercession for the lost.

At 7 and 10 a.m. on Sunday morning and after the evening services from 9 to 11 p.m. they prayed on month after month until, for over a year before the revival finally came, some two hundred people would be present at a nightly prayer-meeting. Was it any wonder that their burden for the priceless souls of men and women increased to boiling point? Souls were being frequently saved, but the praying group was not satisfied. They longed for a letting loose of the heavenly floodtides.

At the beginning of 1905 they brought in an accredited evangelist, but his preaching did not usher in the revival. A jealous God was ready to work in His own time and way through His chosen, praying channels. Just one more right choice and the revival would be upon them. The church decided to pray on. Meanwhile, they sent their pastor who was in poor health to Bournemouth to recuperate. He stayed but one day. The sight of so many people in wheelchairs made him worse, he said. Instead, he went to South Wales where the Welsh Revival was in progress. What he saw there whetted his appetite for the final touch. After two weeks of keen observation and heart-searching, he returned to Edinburgh to report what had most deeply stirred his own soul. It was the final heavenly breeze that fanned the smouldering sparks into a conflagration and revival had indeed at last come to Charlotte Chapel.

Revival! That glorious word! How often do we long and pray for it! How many times do Christians dream of it! But what does it mean when it actually comes? A study of the revival at Charlotte Chapel, Edinburgh, 1905-1907, should be an encouragement and a challenge to every evangelical congregation in the land.

But are we willing? The prophet asks, "Who shall abide the day of His coming?" It is truly an awe-inspiring occasion when God by His Holy Spirit sweeps in upon a people. We quote from an eye-witness account of the Charlotte Chapel revival:

"The meetings on Lord's Day were marked by an earnest outgoing of the soul to God in prayer, and a passionately expressed desire for the salvation of men, all of which told of the dealings many had had—Jacob-like—with God alone. It was, however, at a late prayer-meeting, held in the evening at 9:30, that the fire of God fell. There was nothing, humanly speaking, to account for what happened. Quite suddenly, upon one and another came an overwhelming sense of the reality and awfulness of His presence and of eternal things. Life, death, and eternity seemed suddenly laid bare. Prayer and weeping began, and gained in intensity every moment. As on the day of laying the foundation of the second temple, 'the people could not discern the noise of the shout of joy from the noise of the weeping of the people' (Ezra 3:13). One was overwhelmed before the sudden bursting of the bounds."

May we never lose sight of the fact that a revival begins with Christians. Indeed, it is the Church that must needs be revived. Sinners are dead in their trespasses and sins. They can be reached and brought in by revival. New converts are the fruit of such a work. But it is at the house of God where judgment always begins. So it was in this case. What had transformed this not-long-since empty church into a scene like this? The house was full, or nearly so, largely of Christians. And how God was working on their hearts!

"The Chapel was opened all day on the 1st January, and meetings were held at 11, 3, and 6:30. At every meeting, especially in the afternoon and evening, God drew near. The afternoon meeting got entirely beyond a cut-and-dried program, and resolved itself into one of prayer, confession, testimony, and praise. Testimonies from friends at home and visitors from a distance were given to the fresh power which had come into their lives. The evening meeting went on without the guidance of any human hand; and though friends were present who had been engaged to address it, no address could be given. The people were bowed in prayer, heart-searching, and contrition. And it was only while thus waiting that light broke in upon many hearts, once more revealing and bringing to light the 'hidden things of darkness' and compelling separation from sin unto God. During the meetings a number of unconverted persons decided for Christ; but the burden of all the meetings was that 'Judgment must begin at the house of God.'

"Believers have been awakened to a sense of having lived defeated lives, bound by the 'law of sin and death'; progress retarded by 'weights' and 'sins,' spiritual growth stunted by habits of various kinds. Over all these things victory has been claimed. Brethren have been reconciled to one another; differences which kept sisters apart have been destroyed. Many have testified to victory over novel-reading, dancing, theater-going, etc. Beyond our ordinary services on Lord's Day, there has been very little or no preaching. While the work has been chiefly confined to the saints of God, purifying, humbling, purging, cleansing, there have been numerous conversions. But these have all taken place during the time of prayer, and prayer usually of a tumultuous sort."

What an overhauling we all undergo when ushered into God's Holy presence! We cannot go into His audience chamber with petitions for the souls of men without getting within the sound of His voice. And how He does speak, sometimes in that softest of whispers which completely breaks us down, and again in the thundering tones of Divine displeasure that cause us to quickly put our house in order! Doubtless the Judgment Day will reveal that an unwillingness to break down under the mighty hand of God has long held back revival among us. "O God, revive Thy work," the prophet cried, and let us today reecho the plea and add, "Lord, let it begin in me now."

As in all true revivals, a most marked feature in the Charlotte Chapel Revival was the spirit of prayer poured out upon the people:

"The people were now on the tiptoe of expectancy for a revival. A Conference held on January 22nd, 1906, addressed by several workers who had visited Wales, lasted from 3:30 p.m. until midnight. From that day it was felt that the fire of God had fallen; and as far as Charlotte Chapel was concerned, God had answered prayer, and reviving had come. By the end of 1905, the church had been praying one whole year without so much as one solitary break. Night after night, week after week, month after month, the prayer-meetings went on, increasing in numbers and intensity. It is impossible to convey any adequate idea of the prayer passion that characterized those meetings. There was little or no preaching, it being no uncommon experience for the pastor to go to the pulpit on the Lord's Day, and find the congregation so caught in the spirit of prayer as to render preaching out of the question."

We here describe one meeting by quoting from an account by Mr. Kemp:

"Among the many remarkable features of the recent spiritual awakening in our midst none has been more striking than the all-night prayer-meeting held on February 16th. Beginning at ten o'clock on the Saturday night, it continued until eight o'clock on the Lord's Day morning. The only break during the whole night was at two o'clock, when tea was served. Fully two hundred people would be present until that hour, and not fewer than one hundred and fifty remained the whole of the night.

"It is not possible to describe such a meeting. It is necessary to be in it to know it. From the beginning to the close the prayers ascended in one unbroken continuity. At times the prayers rose and fell like the waves of the sea. At half-past three in the morning the scenes were bewildering to behold. It seemed as though everybody in the meeting was praying at once. There was no confusion; nothing unseemly. The passion of prayer had caught the people, and we felt we must pray."

Was it any wonder that hundreds of souls were gathered in? Something like over a thousand enquirers were recorded during this period. How transformed was every aspect of the work! The chapel was at times so packed that people crowded into every available space, overflowing into the aisles and up the pulpit steps. At times the

Christians would be organized into special open-air groups during the preaching, that room might be made for the unconverted. From a struggling congregation that could muster about thirty-five for a Sunday morning service, in two years' time the actual membership had grown to more than 600. Mr. Kemp thus describes a few of the blessed results:

"It is impossible to record in detail the striking incidents of the revival movement of 1905. If its genuineness can be attested by its results, then we need have no doubt regarding it. It has given us a full church night and morning, which of itself is something to be profoundly thankful for in days when it was conceded the churches have lost their hold on the people. It has given us a most loyal and devoted band of workers, whose aim is the glory of God in the salvation of sinners. It has taught us to pray in a fashion few of us knew of before. It has given to both young and old a new love for the Bible. Time would fail to tell of the purified lives, change homes, and the brightened outlook of hundreds."

Meanwhile, a congregational missionary had been called to assist the pastor because of the rapid expansion of the work. Soon after, a deaconess also joined the team. And to look after the rapidly increasing converts, the area was divided into districts and thirty-four volunteer visitors were calling in homes to follow up the good work begun in so many hearts. Soon young people were in training for work in China and India. Ministers from other congregations were in constant attendance and taking back blessing to their own flocks. Eternity alone will reveal what it meant for revival to come to Charlotte Chapel.

In the summer of 1915, a call came to Mr. Kemp to fill the pulpit at Calvary Baptist Church in New York City. Speaking of his former fourteen years of service at Charlotte Chapel he said: "Only those who pass through such years, and do the work, know the tremendous strain upon body and mind. The taut string snaps sooner or later. To slacken off is safety. A prolonged temporary break in the present ministry did not seem possible; and the only alternative was the acceptance of what we are assured is, at this stage, a truly Divine call to another sphere. We seek and feel certain we shall have the prayers of all our people for the work to be taken up in New York at the beginning of October."

He later resigned from Calvary Church and accepted the call to become pastor of the Metropolitan Tabernacle, New York. Here was formed a Bible Training and Missionary Institute, but his work was suddenly terminated because of a total breakdown which necessitated his resignation. For a whole year he had had distressing symptoms which issued in his near fatal seizure. The Doctor had asked for two years' rest, but after one year his health was so much improved that he undertook a pastorate in Auckland, New Zealand. The sea voyage aided much in his restoration to health so in 1920 he undertook the work at New Zealand Baptist Church. Here he founded the New Zealand Bible Training Institute.

His Bible studies were greatly appreciated, and were sent out as a correspondence course by the editor of *Life of Faith* magazine.

At last, on September 4th, 1932, at sixty years of age, Mr. Kemp passed to his reward. The worker in God's harvest-field had performed his task. He will be particularly remembered by that great revival effort the results of which, A. C. Dixon felt, were more lasting and far-reaching than those of the Welsh Revival.

Chapter Five

MOODY AND HIS INTERCESSORS

Men favored of God have been those whose passion was to know God. They loved the Scriptures and let God reveal Himself through the only remaining record which sets forth His attributes. As a result of that intimate knowledge they were emboldened to spend much time in secret in meditation, prayer, and intercession.

Let us acquaint ourselves with the private, devotional life of just one such man, Dwight L. Moody. We are told that he rose regularly at four o'clock in the morning that he might have at least a full hour with God in prayer and with the Bible before anybody else on the place should be awake. He said, "Next to the wonder of seeing my Savior will be, I think, the wonder that I have made so little of the power of prayer." A personal friend, R. A. Torrey, wrote of Moody's praying and its effects on others:

"The second secret of the great power exhibited in Mr. Moody's life was that Mr. Moody was in the deepest and most meaningful sense a man of prayer. . . . D. L. Moody certainly was a wonderful preacher; taking it all in all. . . . But out of a very intimate acquaintance with him I wish to testify that he was a far great pray-er than he was preacher. Time and time again, he was confronted by obstacles that seemed insurmountable, but he always knew the way to overcome all difficulties. He knew the way to bring to pass anything that needed to be brought to pass. He knew and believed in the deepest depths of his soul that 'nothing was too hard for the Lord' and that prayer could do anything that God could do.

"Oftentimes Mr. Moody would write me when he was about to undertake some new work, saying, 'I am beginning work in such and such a place on such and such a day; I wish you would get the students together for a day of fasting and prayer'; and often I have taken those letters and read them to the students in the lecture room far into the night—sometimes till one, two, three, four, or even five o'clock in the morning, crying to God just because Mr. Moody urged us to wait upon God until we received His blessing."

Thirteen years before Moody was evangelizing England and Scotland, a Christian business man said of him, "If God can use that instrument, He can use anybody." And so He can, if that anybody will learn the same secret of power—the power of prayer.

It was not, then, Moody's talents or educational advantages that rendered him so useful, but the tremendous, moving force that prayer became in his life—not only in personal intercession but by God moving individuals in various parts of the world to intercede on behalf of his ministry. Indeed, perhaps few public figures in the last two centuries have had more interesting records of intercessors who, moved by a divine hand, helped make public efforts so productive of good. Why was this so? Because God had found a man whose will was completely His and who gave Him all the glory. In his sixties, Moody was asked what was the principal event for good in his life. "Well, a good many events have been for good, but perhaps none better than the surrender of my will to God," he replied.

Truth is stranger than fiction, and a real life story is more fascinating than any plot concocted by a writer. Especially is this the case when a person is in touch with the Almighty God as was D. L. Moody. "God plants His footsteps on the sea and rides upon the storm," said the hymn writer. To trace these footsteps of the invisible God Who is never far from anyone of us is entrancing, but it needs an anointed eye to recognize, in providences, the Almighty riding majestically even above the storms of life.

Intriguing to the reader of biography is the way in which God moved people, continents apart, through unpleasant circumstances, to intercede for those they had never seen. Events which seem but ordinary or tragic happenings, viewed in the light of God's eternal purposes, are strangely interwoven with the efforts of fully abandoned laborers in God's vast harvest. Prayer, when motivated by the Holy Spirit, has always been closely allied with the movements of God in the salvation of souls or the deepening of His saints.

Let us trace, then, the footsteps of the Almighty in the lives of Moody's faithful intercessors and discover God's methods in getting them to the right place both spiritually and geographically, where they could uphold His faithful servant in constant, believing prayer.

Sarah Cooke and Mrs. Hawxhurst

Sarah Cooke was one such pray-er and it was she who was used of God to lead Moody into a deeper abandonment. In middle age, Sarah's husband determined to migrate to America from Olney, England. It was not by chance that he entered into business partnership with a relative in the Midwest, in the city of Chicago. This brought Sarah Cooke, hungry for more of God, to this part of the American continent. Soon she was attending a camp-meeting nearby where she was attracted by the joyous faces of those possessing an experience which she had never known. Seeking earnestly, she received a baptism in the Holy Ghost in June, 1871.

A second providence, this time a seemingly tragic one, caused a widow woman, Mrs. Hawxhurst, to leave her elegant home in Brooklyn, New York, and transfer residence to the Chicago area to be near relatives. Here she began a work among the poorer classes. Meeting Mrs. Cooke one day after a noon prayer meeting, the two combined in their efforts for God. But we will let Mrs. Cooke tell the story in her own words taken from her book entitled *Wayside Sketches:*

"I came to Chicago in the year 1868 a perfect stranger. My husband and his brother had been here some time before and from the window of my first home on Wabash Avenue I would watch the multitudes coming and going and often wondered where I would find my work to do for God. The first place I found was the Y.M.C.A. Their rooms then were located on Madison St., near La Salle Street. Mr. Moody was an active worker there—'a diamond in the rough'—most truly, with one desire to do good burning through everything, his very earnestness moving the people, but withal such a lack in his teachings of the divine unction and power. He was always kind and friendly and anxious to enlist in any way the help of Christians. He always encouraged me to take part in his meetings.

"It was at the St. Charles camp-meeting in 1871 that a burden came on me for Mr. Moody, a travail of soul deeper than I have ever had for any other being on God's earth, that the Lord would give him the Baptism of the Holy Ghost and of fire. No opportunity after that was lost in urging upon him his great need and encouraging him to seek with the certainty that it was for him.

"In Mr. Moody's meetings Mrs. Hawxhurst and I were almost always together. . . . At first as we talked with Mr. Moody, there was no antagonism—but little conviction of his need of any further work. However, he asked us to meet with him at Farwel Hall every Friday afternoon which we did for a number of weeks. As we met there from time to time, he would get increasingly in earnest, and the last Friday preceding our great Chicago fire in 1871, he was intensely so. This was during the month of October.

"At each meeting each of us prayed aloud in turn, but at this meeting Mr. Moody's agony was so great that he rolled on the floor and in the midst of many tears and groans cried to God to be baptized with the Holy Ghost and fire. . . ."

The following Sunday evening Chicago became engulfed in flames which consumed a large portion of this city's buildings. The home of Sarah Cooke and Moody's church were fuel for the devouring fire, and only ashes remained, save what they had been enabled to salvage of personal belongings.

We had often wondered why Wall Street, New York, was the place of Moody's baptism, when he labored in Chicago, but he had gone to that metropolis to solicit funds for a new building. Mrs. Cooke takes up the story again:

"After the great fire, Mr. Moody went to New York to solicit funds for the rebuilding of his institutions but he said his heart was not in it. The great cry of his soul was for the Baptism of the Holy Ghost. While on Wall Street, it fell upon him just as on the first disciples and with the same glorious results. From this time he rapidly became famous in his work for God, and two years after, in connection with Mr. Sankey, he went to England."

We have read the account as written by Mrs. Cooke and how she was led to pray for Mr. Moody, but let us ponder Mr. Moody's own words about this important preparation for revival work. He had watched those two women sitting in his services and knew by their countenances that they were praying for him, but he wondered why he was the subject of their concern.

"I need the power?" he queried. "Why? I thought I had the power. I had the largest congregations in Chicago, and there were many conversions. I was in a sense satisfied. But right along these two godly women kept praying for me, and their earnest talk about anointing for special service set me to thinking. There came a great hunger into my soul. I really felt that I did not want to live if I could not have this power for service.

"My heart was not in the work of begging. I could not appeal. I was crying all the time that God would fill me with His Spirit. Well, one day, in the city of New York—oh, what a day!—I cannot describe it. I seldom refer to it; it is almost too sacred an experience to name. I can only say that God revealed Himself to me, and I had such an experience of His love that I had to ask Him to stay His hand. I went to preaching again. The sermons were not different; I did not present any new truths, and yet hundreds were converted. I would not now be placed back where I was before that blessed experience if you should give me all the world—it would be as the small dust of the balance."

Sitting in his old church, in the last year of his life, unfaded memories flooded in upon Mr. Moody as he traced once again God's footsteps in his life, which had led him so providentially across the ocean to yet another sphere of fruitful ministry. S. D. Gordon, who was interviewing him, has preserved for us these vivid recollections of those momentous months following the Chicago fire.

"'This building was not yet up far enough to do much in,' he said; 'so I thought I would slip across the water, and learn what I could from preachers there, so as to do better work here. I got over to London, and was running around after men there.'

"He had not been speaking anywhere, he said, but listening to others. One day, Saturday, at noon, he had gone into the meeting in Exeter Hall on the Strand. He felt impelled to speak a little when the meeting was thrown open, and did so. A minister at the close greeted him, and asked him to come and preach for him the next day, morning and night. He said he would. Mr. Moody said, 'I went to the morning service and found a large church full of people. And when the time came I began to speak to them. But it seemed the hardest talking ever I did. There was no response on their faces. They seemed as though carved out of stone or ice. And I was having a hard time. I wished I wasn't there and I wished I hadn't promised to speak again at night. But I had promised, and so I went.

"'At night it was the same thing. The house was full and people were outwardly respectful, but there was no interest and no response. I was having a hard time again. When about halfway through my talk there came a change. It seemed as though the windows of Heaven had opened and a bit of breath blew down. The atmosphere of the building seemed to change. The people's faces changed. It impressed me so that when I finished speaking I gave the invitation for those who wanted to be Christians to rise. I thought there might be a few. To my immense surprise the people got up in groups, pews-full.

"'I turned to the minister and said, "What does this mean?"

"'He said, "I don't know, I'm sure."

"'Well,' Mr. Moody continued, 'they misunderstood me. I'll explain what I meant.'

"So he announced an after-meeting in the room below, explaining who were invited: only those who wanted to be Christians. Putting pretty clearly what he understood that to mean, he dismissed the service.

"They went to the lower room. And the people came crowding in below, filling all available spaces, seats, aisles, and standing room. Mr. Moody talked again a few minutes, and then asked those who would be Christians to rise. This time he knew he had made his meaning clear. They got up in clumps, in groups, by fifties.

"Mr. Moody said, 'I turned and said to the minister, "What *does* this mean?"

"'He said, "I'm sure I don't know." He continued, "What'll I do with them? This is something new."

"'Well!' Mr. Moody said, 'I'd announce a meeting for tomorrow night, and Tuesday night, and see what comes of it. I'm going across the channel to Dublin.'

"He went, but he had hardly stepped off the boat when a cablegram was handed him from the minister saying, 'Come back at once. Church packed.'

"So he went back and stayed ten days. The result of that ten days, as I recall Mr. Moody's words, was that four hundred were added to that church, and that every church nearby felt the impulse of those ten days. Then Mr. Moody dropped his head as though thinking back and said, 'I had no plans beyond this church. I supposed my life work was here. But the result with me was that I was given a roving commission and have been working under it ever since.'

"Now what was the explanation of that marvelous Sunday and days following? It was not Mr. Moody's doing, though he was a leader whom God could and did mightily use. It was not the minister's doing; for he was as greatly surprised as the leader. There was some secret, hidden beneath the surface of those ten days. With his usual keenness Mr. Moody set himself to ferret it out.

A Nameless Intercessor

"By and by this incident came to him. A member of the church, a woman, had been taken sick some time before. Then she grew worse. The physician told her she would not recover. That is, she would not die at once, so far as he could judge, but she would be shut in her home for years. And she thought of her life, and said, 'How little I've done for God: practically nothing. Now what can I do, shut in here on my back?' And she said, 'I can pray. I will pray.'

"She was led to pray for her church. Her sister, also a member of the church, lived with her, and was her link with the outer world. Sundays, after church service, the sick woman would ask, 'Any special interest in church today?'

"'No,' was the constant reply. Wednesday nights, after prayer-meetings, she would again inquire, 'Any special interest in the service tonight?'

"'No, nothing new; same old deacons made the same old prayers.'

"But one Sunday noon the sister came in from service and asked, 'Who do you think preached today?'

"'I don't know; who?'

"'Why, a stranger from America—a man called Moody, I think was the name.'

"The sick woman's face turned a bit whiter, and her eyes looked half scared. Her lips trembled as she quietly said: 'I know what that means. There's something coming to the old church. Don't bring me any dinner. I must spend the afternoon in prayer.' And that night in the service that startling change came.

"Then to Mr. Moody himself, as he sought her out in her sick room, she told how nearly two years before there came into her hands a copy of a paper published in Chicago, called the *Watchman*. It contained a talk by Mr. Moody. All she knew was that that talk made her heart burn, and there was the name M-o-o-d-y. She was led to simply pray that God would send that man into their church in London.

"The months went by, and a year, and over; still she prayed. Nobody knew of it but herself and God. No change seemed to come. Still she prayed, and of course her prayer wrought its purpose—every Spirit-suggested prayer does. The Spirit of God moved that man of God across the water and into London, and into their church. Then there was her special siege-prayer, a sort of last charge up the steep hill, and that night the victory came.

"I believe without a doubt that some day when the night is gone, and the morning light comes up, and we know as we are known, we shall find that the largest single factor, in that ten days' work, and in the changing of tens of thousands of lives under Moody's leadership is that woman in her praying. Not the only factor, mind you, for Moody was a man of rare leadership and consecration, and hundreds of faithful ministers and others rallied to his support.

"Yet I do not know her name. I know Mr. Moody's name. I could name scores of faithful men associated with him in his campaign, but the name of this one in whom humanly is the secret of it all I do not know. Ah! It is a secret service."

A Group of Pray-ers

Again, later, while undertaking a campaign at Cambridge, we see how inspired intercessory prayer routed the devil's opposition. Moody tells of this campaign:

"I don't think the preaching had anything to do with it. Mr. Sankey and I had a pressing invitation to go to Cambridge when we were in England ten years ago, and I refused. I thought I had no call to go to universities. But when we were over there again, another call came, signed by a list of names six or eight feet long, and I said, 'I will go.'

"The first Sunday night we were in Cambridge the students tried to break up the meeting. I had preached to all classes of people—to hoodlums and all—and never had that happened before. It looked very much as if they were going to snatch the whole thing out of our hands. I don't think there were fifty students out of that roomful that heard the songs of Mr. Sankey, and right on through the whole meeting it was just the same.

"On Monday night the disturbance was just as bad, or worse. On Tuesday the outlook was darker than ever. But on that day a lady, a bedridden saint, who was very much interested in the work, sent around word to a few Christians to get together in a little upper room, to plead with God for a change in those students. That turned the tide. It wasn't the preaching. They had heard better sermons from the best preachers in England. It was those Christians, in that upper room, praying to God, that made the difference. And how they did pray! It seemed as if their prayers burst into Heaven, and I said, 'The victory is ours.'

"The next Sunday night there were two or three hundred inquirers—men of broken hearts, crying out for God. It isn't preaching we want. It is prayer. I would rather be able to pray like Daniel than to preach like Gabriel. We don't want any more preachers in this country, we have enough. What we want is to pray. Let us open up communication with Heaven, and the blessing will come down."

        ***   ***   ***

Another author, R. D. Johnston, gives a further insight into Moody's campaigns at both Oxford and Cambridge. We are given, perhaps, a clearer picture of the opposition encountered and the victory obtained:

"In both places, out of hectic and hilarious times, came Heaven-born blessing, and not for the first time in the history of Gospel preaching, was it found that 'fools who came to scoff remained to pray.' But the efforts taxed the grace and courage of the evangelist to the utmost. 'Well, Sankey, I guess I've no hankering after that crowd again!' said

Moody, after the opening Cambridge meeting, as in his hotel he took off his dripping collar. Yet a few nights later was saved, among others, one of the ringleaders of the Sunday night demonstration, who had excused his rowdyism with the remark: 'If uneducated men will come to teach the 'Varsity, they deserve to be snubbed.' From that night Gerard Lander took a leading place in the spiritual life of Cambridge, and became, in after years, Bishop of Hong Kong.

"So bad was their reception at the hands of the Oxford students that Mr. Moody felt it imperative to administer a cutting rebuke. 'We came to this city,' he said, 'expecting to meet the flower of British gentry. I put it to you, gentlemen, have you treated us strangers with ordinary courtesy? Whatever you may think of us and our message, we demand that you should behave at least as gentlemen towards us.'

"At the close of the service a number waited and tendered apologies that would have satisfied an ordinary man. These Mr. Moody declined, in a characteristic reply: 'No, gentlemen, I will not accept your apologies unconditionally. You have treated us in a manner beneath contempt. Your discourtesy has been public; your apology must be public too. I will reserve three rows of seats in the front of the audience for tomorrow night's meeting, and if you will attend, occupy these seats, and allow me to inform the audience that your presence there is your apology, Mr. Sankey and I will accept it.'

"To a man they came, and sat while Mr. Moody explained matters to a tense audience, finishing it with: 'I'm much obliged to you, gentlemen, for giving me a hearing; there are thirty or forty of you here who promised me you'd come tonight and listen fair, and you've done it. I'm much obliged.'"

Statistics never bothered Moody. When a fellow-minister asked how many converts had been saved under his ministry, he replied, "I don't know anything about that, doctor. Thank God, I don't have to. I don't keep the Lamb's Book of Life."

One day, however, this Book will reveal in full the blessings radiating from the efforts of those who gave themselves to prayer and the ministry in Moody's day. These cannot be calculated until the final records are made up in the ages to come.

Chapter Six

FINNEY AND HIS INTERCESSORS

"Strong, vigorous converts are born into the Kingdom when there has been wrestling with God on the part of some one," said Charles G. Finney, surely an authority on revivals and results.

We are convinced through extensive research and study into biography and the history of revivals that genuine Spirit-wrought results always can be traced to seasons of extraordinary prayer on the part of private individuals or of a church or group united in prayer. We have concluded that intercession and the Spirit's response are inseparable twins.

Mr. Finney, in the accompanying paragraph taken from his *Revival Lectures,* expresses a similar conviction: "Prayer is an essential link in the chain of causes that lead to a revival; as much so as truth is. Some have zealously used truth to convert men and laid very little stress on prayer. They have preached and talked and distributed tracts with great zeal and then wondered that they had so little success.

"The reason was that they forgot to use the other branch of the means, effectual prayer. They overlooked the fact that truth by itself will never produce the effect because it will not be believed without the Spirit of God."

Perhaps since the days of St. Paul, no one has more championed the cause of prevailing prayer than Charles G. Finney, both in his preaching and in his lectures which come down to us through his books. His legal mind demolishes all excuses. But he learned what he did of prayer in the school of prayer itself. "In regard to my own experience," said the revivalist, "I will say that unless I had the spirit of prayer I could do nothing. If even for a day or an hour I lost the spirit of grace and supplication, I found myself unable to preach with power and efficiency, or to win souls by personal conversation...."

"Sometimes I would find myself, in a great measure, empty of this power. I would go out and visit, and find that I had made no saving impression. I would exhort and pray with the same result. I would then set apart a day for private fasting and prayer, fearing that this power had departed from me, and would enquire anxiously after the reason of this apparent emptiness. After humbling myself, and crying out for help, the power would return upon me with all its freshness. This has been the experience of my life.

"For several weeks, I was very strongly exercised in prayer, and had an experience that was somewhat new to me. I found myself so much exercised, and so borne down with the weight of immortal souls, that I was constrained to pray without ceasing. Some of my experiences, indeed, alarmed me. A spirit of importunity sometimes came upon me so that I would say to God that He had made a promise to answer prayer, and I could not, and would not, be denied. I felt so certain that He would hear me, and that faithfulness to His promises and to Himself, rendered it impossible that He should not hear and answer, that frequently I found myself saying to Him, 'I hope Thou dost not think that I can be denied. I come with Thy faithful promises in my hand, and I cannot be denied.'

"I cannot tell how absurd unbelief looked to me, and how certain it was, in my mind, that God would answer prayer—those prayers that, from day to day, and from hour to hour, I found myself offering in such agony and faith."

Father Nash

When God possesses a man fully for His divine purposes, He often inspires and calls others to assist by interceding in prayer. Two ministers gave up their public ministry for a season in order to engage in prayer for the services. One such was Father Nash. In a letter written by Mr. Finney to the Rev. P. C. Headley, he introduces us to this prayerful figure:

"Dear Brother:

"The first time I ever saw Rev. Daniel Nash was at the meeting of the presbytery which licensed me to preach the Gospel. Soon after that he was confined to his room with disease of his eyes, and was almost entirely blind for about six months. During this period he gave himself to much prayer, and had a great searching and overhauling in his spiritual life, and, before he could see enough to be abroad, was powerfully baptized with the Holy Ghost.

"Soon after this he came to me in the midst of a powerful revival of religion. I could not fail to see that he had been made over, and was quite another man. He was full of the Holy Ghost. He had the strongest faith, and was the mightiest man of prayer that I had at that time ever seen. Afterwards he labored with me in revivals in Govereur and DeKalb. In the midst of the great revival in Rome, Oneida, he came to me and labored in prayer and conversation with great effect. He followed me to Utica, and afterwards in Troy and New Lebanon.

"He was a most wonderful man in prayer, one of the most earnest, devout, spiritually-minded, heavenly-minded men I ever saw. He labored about in many places in central and northern New York, and gave himself up to almost constant prayer, literally praying himself to death at last. He was found dead in his room in the attitude of prayer.

"While I was laboring in Boston in the winter of 1831, I wrote asking him to join with me in keeping every Friday as a day of fasting and prayer, for the more general outpouring of the Holy Spirit. He replied that his body was nearly worn out, that the Holy Spirit had laid the world upon his heart and pressed him almost to death.

"Those that knew him, during the period of which I speak, will never forget his prayers, and the unutterable groaning with which he was exercised by the Holy Spirit. The manifest and instantaneous answer to some of his prayers was so startling as to arrest the attention of everybody about him. He lived but a few years after I became acquainted with him, but what years those were, and what a life was that! He lived almost in Heaven.

"I have seen him for days in a state of mind so joyful and triumphant that his face literally shone with the joy of his soul. At those seasons he would say to me, 'Brother Finney, I cannot pray; my soul is so full of Heaven, I can do nothing but praise.' But soon he would come down and take the load of unconverted sinners upon his heart, and such agonizing, prevailing prayers I never heard from any other man.

"Many times in a meeting, his soul would become so full of anguish that he could not remain and keep silent. He would hastily and as quietly as possible retire from the meeting, and seek a place where he could pour out his soul to God; and for hours he would continue to wrestle and agonize, and groan his soul out to God, until his strength was completely exhausted.

"The spirit of prayer that was upon him was quite a stumbling-block to professors of religion who had never known the Holy Ghost as the Spirit that maketh intercession for the saints according to the will of God with groaning that cannot be uttered. I should here say, that very much of this type of prayer prevailed in the revivals through central and northern New York at that time.

"Many lay men and women were exercised in a similar manner, and sometimes would pray all night in their closets with unutterable groaning for the salvation of sinners. It is devoutly to be wished that the Lord would stir up someone to publish a brief history of the spirit of prayer that prevailed in those revivals, with the many wonderful answers that occurred from day to day."

Abel Clary

There was yet another man who also assisted Finney in his effort for souls. In his own words, we are introduced to his prayer-partner in these revival efforts:

"I must introduce the name of a man, whom I shall have occasion to mention frequently, Mr. Abel Clary. He was the son of a very excellent man, and an elder of the church where I was converted. He was converted in the same revival in which I was. He had been licensed to preach; but his spirit of prayer was such, he was so burdened with the souls of men, that he was not able to preach much, his whole time and strength being given to prayer. The burden of his soul would frequently be so great that he was unable to stand, and he would writhe and groan in agony. I was well acquainted with him, and knew something of the wonderful spirit of prayer that was upon him. He was a very silent man, as almost all are who have that powerful spirit of prayer.

"The first I knew of his being at Rochester, a gentleman who lived about a mile west of the city, called on me one day, and asked me if I knew a Mr. Abel Clary, a minister. I told him that I knew him well. 'Well,' said he, 'he is at my house, and has been there for some time, and I don't know what to think of him.'

"'I have not seen him at any of our meetings,' I replied.

"'No,' he replied. 'He cannot go to meeting, he says. He prays nearly all the time, day and night, and in such an agony of mind that I do not know what to make of it. Sometimes he cannot even stand on his knees, but will lie prostrate on the floor, and groan and pray in a manner that quite astonishes me.'

"I said to the brother, 'I understand it; please keep still. It will all come out right; he will surely prevail.'

"I knew at that time a considerable number of men who were exercised in the same way, and a large number of women partook of the same spirit, and spent a great part of their time in prayer.... This Mr. Clary continued in Rochester as long as I did, and did not leave it until after I had left. He never, that I could learn, appeared in public, but gave himself wholly to prayer."

And again Mr. Finney writes of this same Abel Clary: "I have spoken of Mr. Clary as a praying man, who was at Rochester. He had a brother, a physician, living in Auburn. I think it was the second Sabbath that I was at Auburn at this time. I observed in the congregation the solemn face of this Mr. Clary. He looked as if he was borne down with an agony of prayer. Being well acquainted with him, and knowing the great gift of God that was upon him, the spirit of prayer, I was very glad to see him there. He sat in the pew with his brother, the Doctor, who was also a professor of religion, but who knew nothing by experience, I should think, of his brother Abel's great power with God.

"At intermission, as soon as I came down from the pulpit, Mr. Clary, with his brother, met me at the pulpit stairs, and the Doctor invited me to go home with him and spend the intermission and get some refreshments. I did so.

"After arriving at his house, we were soon summoned to the dinner table. We gathered about the table, and Dr. Clary turned to his brother and said, 'Brother Abel, will you ask a blessing.'

"Brother Abel bowed his head and began, audibly, to ask a blessing. He had uttered but a sentence or two when he broke down, moved suddenly back from the table, and fled to his chamber. The Doctor supposed he had been taken suddenly ill, and rose up and followed him. In a few minutes he came down and said, 'Mr. Finney, Brother Abel wants to see you.'

"Said I, 'What ails him?'

"Said he, 'I do not know; but he says you know. He appears in great distress, but I think it is the state of his mind.'

"I understood it in a moment and went to his room. He lay groaning upon the bed, the Spirit making intercession for him and in him with groaning that could not be uttered. I had barely entered the room, when he made out to say, 'Pray, Brother Finney.' I knelt down and helped him in prayer by leading his soul out for the conversion of sinners. I continued to pray until his distress passed away.

"I understood that this was the voice of God. I saw the spirit of prayer was upon him, and I felt His influence upon myself, and took it for granted that the work would move on powerfully. It did so. I believe, but am not quite sure, that every one of those men that signed that paper, making a long list of names, were converted during that revival."

Mr. Finney himself

In the latter part of his life when strength was failing and the cause of revivals looked very dismal indeed, Finney, himself, had another season of agonizing prayer. This preceded and ushered in a period of extraordinary blessing as unexpectedly the Lord opened up a door of usefulness to him wider than any he had hitherto experienced. While traveling on a steamer, the mind of this revivalist became agitated so that he could do little but pace the deck and cabin in agonizing intercession. Out of that travail was born his most enduring work—the publishing of his lectures on the subject of revivals. He shares with us the happenings of that eventful day.

"Returning from a sea voyage, my mind became exceedingly exercised on the question of revivals. I feared that they would decline throughout the country. I feared that the opposition that had been made to them had grieved the Holy Spirit. My own health, it appeared to me, had nearly or quite broken down; and I knew of no other evangelist that would take the field, and aid pastors in revival work.

"This view of the subject distressed me so much that one day I found myself unable to rest. My soul was in an utter agony. I spent almost the entire day in prayer in my stateroom, or walking the deck in intense agony, in view of the state of things. In fact I felt crushed with the burden that was on my soul. There was no one on board to whom I could open my mind, or say a word.

"It was the spirit of prayer that was upon me; that which I had often experienced in kind, but perhaps never before to such a degree, for so long a time. I besought the Lord to go on with His work, and to provide Himself with such instrumentalities as were necessary.

"After a day of unspeakable wrestling and agony in my soul, just at night, the subject cleared up to my mind. The Holy Spirit led me to believe that all would come out right, and that God had yet a work for me to do; that I might be at rest; that the Lord would go forward with His work, and give me strength to take any part in it that He desired. But I had not the least idea what the course of His providence would be. (Isaiah 66:8).

"On arriving at New York I found the mob excitement on the subject of slavery very intense. I remained but a day or two in New York, and went into the country. On my return to New York, Mr. Leavitt came to me and said:

"'Brother Finney, I have ruined *The Evangelist* (a religious periodical). I have not been as prudent as you cautioned me to be, and I have gone so far ahead of public intelligence and feeling on the subject of slavery that my subscription list is rapidly falling; and we shall not be able to continue its publication beyond the first of January, unless you can do something to bring the paper back to public favor again.'

"I told him my health was such that I did not know what I could do; but I would make it a subject of prayer. He said if I could write a series of articles on revivals, he had no doubt it would restore the paper immediately to public favor.

"After considering it a day or two, I proposed to preach a course of lectures on revivals of religion, which he might report for his paper. He caught at this at once. Said he, 'That is the very thing.' And in the next number of his paper he advertised the course of lectures.

"This had the effect he desired, and he soon after told me that the subscription list was very rapidly increasing; and, stretching out his long arms, he said, 'I have as many new subscribers every day as would fill my arms with papers, to supply them each a single number.'

"I began the course of lectures immediately, and continued them through the winter, preaching one each week. Mr. Leavitt could not write shorthand but would sit and take notes.

"These lectures were afterward published in a book called, *Finney's Lectures on Revivals*. Twelve thousand copies of them were sold, as fast as they could be printed.

"These revival lectures, meager as was the report of them, and feeble as they were in themselves, have been instrumental, as I have learned, in promoting revivals in England, and Scotland and Wales, on the Continent in various places, in Canada, East and West, in Nova Scotia, and in some of the islands of the sea.

"In England and Scotland, I have often been refreshed by meeting with ministers and laymen, in great numbers, that had been converted directly or indirectly through the instrumentality of those lectures.

" . . . But this was not of man's wisdom. Let the reader remember that long day of agony and prayer at sea, that God would do something to forward the work of revivals, and enable me, if He desired to do it, to take such a course as to help forward the work.

"I felt certain then that my prayers would be answered; and I have regarded all that I have since been able to accomplish, as in a very important sense, an answer to the prayers of that day."

B. T. Roberts comments on the fruitfulness of this printing venture: "New subscribers came in at the rate of sixty a day. The lectures were published in a book, and twelve thousand copies were sold as fast as they could be got ready. They were circulated in England, etc. . . . One publisher in London issued eighty thousand copies. They were translated into French, German, and Welsh. Wherever they went they were the means of promoting revivals of religion."

A student of Oberlin College, forty-five years later, revealed Mr. Finney as a praying man even in his teaching career: "The class in Theology in 1838, met to hear one of the last lectures of the course. Our teacher, as usual, knelt with us in offering the opening prayer. But the burden on his soul for us, for Zion, for a lost world, could not be thrown off in a few petitions. He 'stood in the gap' and wrestled for the blessing. For a whole hour he led us up to God. We then arose and went in profound silence to our rooms. There was no lecture on that day. That prayer, never can we forget it!"

The good Book tells us that "the Spirit maketh intercession for us with groanings which cannot be uttered for we know not how to pray" otherwise. But the Bible also tells us that "no man stirred up himself to pray." There is a personal desire to be moved to such prayer, and then not knowing how to pray, the Spirit will assist us in so sacred a task as bringing men and women to Christ.

Chapter Seven

FRASER OF LISULAND

Life seemed to hold much in store for the twenty-year-old scholar. An excellent student at a London university, he had bright prospects, and each new crossroads in his career seemed to welcome him with a green light. But someone handed James Fraser a little leaflet on missions, and the words arrested the young enthusiast. Somehow he could not push aside the insistence of those words: "If our Master returned today to find millions of people unevangelized, and looked, as of course He would look, to us for an explanation, I cannot imagine what explanation we should have to give. Of one thing I am certain— that most of the excuses we are accustomed to make with such good conscience now, we shall be wholly ashamed of then."

Would he, James, choose to live a normal life in that large city of London, now and again entertaining cultured audiences with his brilliant piano concerts? Would he utilize his degree in Engineering and have ample means to live comfortably and respectably? Or would he lose himself in the remote mountainous regions of China, where many of his talents would be unappreciated? The question continued to weigh heavily upon his young mind. Was it God's call? Was it his mother's prayers that one of her children should be a foreign missionary? Or was it just his own fancy? These all had to be weighed seriously. And the young man did just that. The result was a decision to fulfil the command of the Lord of the Harvest in the seeming waste of his life for those unfortunate, illiterate peoples.

This youth, rich in natural attainments, did not turn away sorrowfully as had the rich young ruler; on the contrary, he gave to God not only the "latch key but the master key of his whole being." Now he was to be under the control of Jesus Christ with no divided allegiances. A new dimension of Christian experience came to this young, prospective missionary. His mother, writing of this experience, said: "He did not talk much about it but I have seen his face shining when he came down from prayer. He said it was that Book which made plain to him his path of duty. Of course, the sacrifice was a real one. He must have known that he had good prospects. He could not but feel his power. But he turned from it all without reserve to consecrate his life to God. Conversion should be a real giving of ourselves, should it not? When that takes place, the Holy Spirit fills the heart and there is joy."

His degree—a B.Sc. in engineering—was taken with honors, and although only twenty-one, this disciple of Jesus Christ lost no time in applying to the China Inland Mission. He spent a year in training, at which time he became more thoroughly acquainted with the Bible and grew to know the history of the Mission to which he had applied. It was based on faith with no appeal for funds publicly. This all appealed to young Fraser. Again the mother gives us an insight into the depth of experience through which her son passed:

"After Jim's conversion, we had such deep, spiritual fellowship. He was a great help to me. We shared spiritual experiences. Indeed, he became my teacher. My progress has been gradual through the years; he seemed a mature Christian right away. He had so completely given himself to the Lord that he could be filled with the Spirit. He emptied himself—and so the Lord could fill him.

"I could not pour the ointment on His blessed feet, as Mary did—but I gave Him my boy," said this dedicated mother whose prayers proved to be a great blessing to her son while separated from her by thousands of miles, often laboring on difficult terrain and at times under most dangerous circumstances. How much he appreciated it might be summed up in the words of his biographer: "Fraser admitted that there were two people to whom he owed everything—D. E. Hoste and his own mother; these two people were notable for their prayer-life, the mother having led a prayer group at home to intercede for the work of her son."

His exploits over some thirty years can best be summed up in the words of St. Paul, the first missionary: "In journeyings often, in perils of waters, in perils of robbers . . . in perils by the heathen . . . in perils in the wilderness . . . in perils among false brethren; in weariness and painfulness, in watchings often, in hunger and thirst, in fastings often, in cold and nakedness. Beside those things that are without, that which cometh upon me daily, the care of all the churches" (II Cor. 11:26-28).

The Overseas Missionary Fellowship, formerly known as The China Inland Mission, had this to say about J. O. Fraser, who has now gone to his reward: "After Hudson Taylor and his biographers, Dr. and Mrs. Howard Taylor, there has been no member of the CIM/OMF with a greater spiritual contribution to the Church. Supremely wise and successful in his church-planting among the Lisu people of southwest China, J. O. Fraser's personal meditations on prayer—shared with friends at home—continue their profound ministry and are in constant demand."

Limited for space, we have concentrated on the prayer-life of this warrior, culling extracts from his own booklet, *The Prayer of Faith,* and also from the two biographies—Mrs. Howard Taylor's *Behind the Ranges,* and his daughter's more recent biography, *Mountain Rain.*

We share these with you in the sincere hope that the Church today may be inspired to sacrifice time and energy consumed on lesser good, in order to prove once again the power and beneficent effects of time spent with God in prayer.

"Finding a place for prayer was often difficult," said his biographer "when he stayed in the huts of the Lisu. Frequently, the mountainside would witness the piercing, importunate pleadings of this man who counted not his prayer-time by minutes but by hours. In the crowded cities, he would find the deserted outer rooms at the back of the temple and there pour out his heart to God in prayer. It was the source of his strength, and he always came back invigorated. Through prayer he had his guidance, and sometimes it seemed like the direct guidance of the Holy Spirit of which the early Quakers used to speak, the leading of the Inner Light."

"I believe that a work of God sometimes goes on behind a particular man or family, village or district, before the knowledge of the truth ever reaches them. It is a silent, unsuspected work, not in mind or heart, but in the unseen realm behind these. Then, when the light of the Gospel is brought, there is no difficulty, no conflict. It is, then, simply a case of 'Stand still, and see the salvation of the Lord.'

"This should give us confidence in praying intelligently for those who are far from the Gospel light. The longer the preparation, the deeper the work. The deeper the root, the firmer the plant when once it springs above ground. I do not believe that any deep work of God takes root without long preparation somewhere...."

"'If two of you shall agree'—I feel even when praying alone, that there are two concerned in the prayer. God and myself...I do not think that a petition which misses the mind of God will ever be answered (I John 5:14). Personally, I feel the need of trusting Him to lead me in prayer as well as in other matters. I find it well to preface prayer not only by meditation, but by the definite request that I may be directed into the channels of prayer to which the Holy Spirit is beckoning me.

"With The Understanding Also. Always remember, 'I will pray with the spirit and I will pray with the understanding also' (I Cor. 14:15). Let the spirit and the understanding work in about equal proportions. First, think over the needs, taking into account any consciousness of spirit-burden. Pray, tentatively, along that line, asking God continually to focus your prayers. If, after covering such ground in prayer, no 'grip' comes anywhere, it is probably best to close down at once. Do not be in a hurry to do this, but don't press on in the energy of the flesh."

"How much of our prayer is of the quality we find in Hannah's 'bitterness of soul,' when she 'prayed unto the Lord?' How many times have we ever 'wept sore' before the Lord? We have prayed much perhaps, but our longings have not been deep as compared with hers. We have spent much time upon our knees, it may be, without our hearts going out in an agony of desire. But real supplication is the child of heartfelt desire, and cannot prevail without it; a desire not of earth nor issuing from our own sinful hearts, but wrought into us by God Himself. Oh, for such desires! Oh for Hannah's earnestness, not in myself only but in all who are joining me in prayer for these poor heathen aborigines!"

"I really believe that if every particle of prayer put up by the home churches on behalf of the infant churches of the mission field were removed, the latter would be swamped by an incoming flood of the powers of darkness. This seems actually to have happened in church history—churches losing all their power and life, becoming a mere empty name, or else flickering out altogether. Just as a plant may die for lack of watering, so may a genuine work of God die and rot for lack of prayer."

"Do you believe that the Church of God would be alive today but for the high-priestly intercession of the Lord Jesus Christ on the throne? I do not; I believe it would have been dead and buried long ago. Viewing the Bible as a record of God's work on this earth, I believe that it gives a clear ringing message to His people—from Genesis to Revelation—YOU DO YOUR PART.

"The breath of God can blow away all those miasmic vapors from the atmosphere of a village, in answer to your prayers. We are not fighting against flesh and blood. You deal with the fundamental issues of this Lisu work when you pray against 'the principalities, the powers, the world rulers of this darkness, the spiritual hosts of wickedness in the heavenlies' (Eph. 6:12)."

"If we grow into spiritual manhood in the spiritual life we shall not escape conflict. As long as Ephesians 6:10-18 remains in the Bible, we must be prepared for serious warfare—'and having done all, to stand.' We must fight through, and then stand victorious on the battlefield.

"Is not this another secret of many unanswered prayers—that they are not fought through? If the result is not seen as soon as expected, Christians are apt to lose heart, and if it is still longer delayed, to abandon it altogether.

"We must count the cost before praying the prayer of faith. We must be willing to pay the price. We must mean business. We must set ourselves to 'see things through with all perseverance.' Our natural strength will fail; and here lies the necessity for a divinely given faith. We can then rest back in the everlasting Arms and renew our strength continually. We can then rest as well as wrestle. In this conflict-prayer, after the definite exercise of faith, there is no need to ask the same thing again and again. It seems to me inconsistent to do so."

"Repeatedly," said Mrs. Howard Taylor, "he had had occasion to notice the difference between people and places that had been much prayed for and those that had not. In the former half, the work seemed to be done already, as if an unseen ally had gone ahead to prepare the way. This made him not only persevere in prayer himself, whether he felt like it or not, but impelled him to induce and encourage Christians at home to pray. He longed for a larger Prayer Circle behind his Lisu work—sent maps of all his districts, wrote personal letters to the members, answered questions, sought in every way to make the needs real to his prayer helpers." (The above quotations have been used with the permission of the Overseas Missionary Fellowship.)

Chapter Eight

MISSIONARIES IN CHINA

Now and again a page from the diary of a missionary appears in a missionary magazine. Perusing such, we have often marveled at the physical constitution that could stand up to such arduous toil and long hours. We admire the tireless worker who unselfishly gives himself without stint for the task, but, we ask ourselves, where is the time to recruit his strength from God's exhaustless resources? Surely, of all people, the missionary surrounded by so much that suggests devil dominion and power, needs much of that calm, unruffled strength that can come only from much time spent with God, gazing until He assumes His proper magnitude and problems their true size. But how little do we bargain with the terrible Satanic powers that seek daily to cut the communication line from the Supply Base to the worker in the strategic center!

William Burns

In this chapter we concentrate particularly on the prayer life of missionaries who labored in China, reserving those of the China Inland Mission for yet another chapter. Let us first look at the life of William Burns, that great man of God. While only around twenty, he began his ministry in Scotland. Daily he prayed for hours that God would give him souls. One morning upon entering his bedroom, his mother found him prostrate on the floor where he had been all night pleading with God for souls. "Mother, God has given me Scotland today!" was his exclamation. Shortly thereafter that area experienced a mighty reviving.

F. S. Arnot, the missionary explorer of Africa, once lodged with elderly folk who had entertained Burns at the time of the outpouring of the Spirit in Robert M'Cheyne's church. They related how on the Saturday before the outpouring, Burns did not come to breakfast. Not liking to disturb him, they waited until the time of the midday meal, at which time he still did not appear. At tea there was as yet no sign of their young guest, so they wondered if he were ill. Gently pushing the door open they found the young preacher stretched out on the floor pleading with God. The next Sabbath, He answered those pleadings with a mighty deluge of grace.

Men of prayer, such as William Burns, discover that even their travels become linked to some chain of providential circumstances which will affect their entire future or the future of those with whom they come in contact. It so happened that Burns came to Aberdeen just when young Andrew and John Murray arrived there from South Africa to pursue their education and were residing with their uncle. The two young Murrays attended the meetings of this fiery revivalist and Andrew made this the deciding time of his life. Doubtless the prayerful preacher impressed something of his own character and image upon the lad who was in the future to have such a wide influence among the churches in South Africa. In his book, *The School of Prayer*, Andrew Murray expresses a wish that there were courses for Christian workers in this neglected art of prayer.

"We are a part of everyone we meet," said a notable minister. How vital then that we contribute to another that which will help him or her become better acquainted with divine things. Young Burns, now a prayer warrior, went to China and God brought him into touch with the youthful Hudson Taylor who was to help shape a continent. Taylor had found that it was "sadly possible to be professedly a witness for Christ amid the darkness of a heathen land and yet breathe little of the love of God or the grace of the Gospel." The lonely young missionary found a kindred spirit in Burns, and looking back upon their companionship together he commented: "His love for the Word was delightful, and his holy, reverential life and constant communing with God made fellowship with him satisfying to the deep cravings of my heart."

There are glimpses in Burns' journal of many a day or night spent in prayer seeking personal holiness, the fundamental requisite for a successful ministry. His biographer, Islay Burns, said, "His whole life was literally a life of prayer, and his whole ministry a series of battles fought at the mercy Seat."

"Who among us has the spirit of prayer?" William wrote from Swatow. "They are mighty who have this spirit, and weak who have it not.... The great fundamental error as far as I can see, in the economy of the Christian life, which many, and alas! I for one commit, is that of having too few and too short periods of solemn retirement with our gracious Father and His adorable Son, Jesus Christ."

"Prayer, unceasing and earnest," Burns again comments, "is that wherein the great strength of a revival of religion lieth."

Simple were the tastes of this man. There were few personal belongings to impede his progress in journeys oft. "I think I can say through grace," he commented, "that God's presence or absence alone distinguishes places to me."

David Hill

We pass on to another notable missionary, David Hill of the Methodist Society, loaned for a period of service to the C. I. M. His life, too, was one of prayer. Knowing that his career would call for arduous travels, this man of God sacrificed marriage because he would have had to divide his allegiance between wife and home and the call of God to pioneer. So this great loving heart gave itself undividedly to others.

W. T. A. Barber, Hill's biographer, writes, "As showing the communion from which he drew his strength for the constant service demanded of him, let us flash a momentary picture on the screen. One night Hill was staying with me. The usual heavy round of unceasing duties sent us wearied to our beds, and ere long I fell asleep. He occupied the next room to mine, and the French windows of our room opened on to the verandah with its outer Venetian shutters. After some hours of sleep, I awoke, to see a broad band of light upon the Venetians opposite me. Fearing fire, I went out on the verandah and looked into his room, from which the light was streaming. The lamp was burning on a table by his bedside; his Greek Testament and notebook lay open. After the day's work he had spent the hours in inmost quiet communion with the Word, till worn out with work, he fell asleep upon his knees, and as the gray morning dawned he was still kneeling as he slept. No strain of daily toil, no weariness, was allowed to justify curtailment of that gazing into the face of Incarnate Love whereby he renewed his strength.

"Even while traveling homeward on furlough, he would, clad in his great-coat, pass hours of the night on the upper deck, drawing strength from on High, like one of those devoted Catholics and Protestants whose lives were to him a study. He was so fearful of becoming too easy in faith and too little in earnest in work, that when considering the Atonement he would give particular attention to what is called the moral side."

When God can find a man of prayer, He often incites others to enter into the spirit of intercession for his work. And God honored David Hill by giving him a convert, Hsi, the Confucian scholar. If Hill's life had been instrumental in bringing only this one man to Christ, it would have been worth the sacrifice.

Mrs. Howard Taylor gives us a glimpse of the prayer behind this striking conversion. "But was it David Hill that won Hsi to Christ? Or was it he alone? Long after both were gone, the writer received the following letter, penned by one of his colleagues at Hankow: 'May I give you an unpublished incident, told me by Mr. Hill himself. "Mr. Hill had a dear friend in England, who was distinguished for her power in prayer. When she died, an unfinished letter was found upon her desk intended for Mr. Hill, and was forwarded to him by the family. In it this lady told Mr. Hill how she had recently been much drawn out in prayer on his behalf, and had specially been led to plead for an extraordinary blessing to be given to him in his work at that time. She felt distinctly that she had been heard, though she knew not what form the blessing would take. The date of this letter was found so closely to correspond with the conversion of Pastor Hsi, that Mr. Hill never doubted that that was the extraordinary blessing given in answer to his friend's prayers."'"

Pastor Hsi

Passing on then from David Hill, let us look at Pastor Hsi of the C.I.M. "Like father, like son," holds spiritually as well as physically. In our brief space here we can but give a very fragmentary glimpse into the inner life of this devoted man. From his biography by Mrs. Howard Taylor, we glean the following sidelights upon his character:

"It was impossible to be with Hsi without having prayer. His first instinct in everything was to turn to God. Long before daylight, those summer mornings, I used to hear him in his room across the courtyard, praying and singing by the hour together. Prayer seemed the very atmosphere of his life, and he expected and received the most evident answers."

Hsi himself records: "On account of many onslaughts of Satan, my wife and I for the space of three years seldom put off our clothing to go to sleep, in order that we might be the more ready to watch and pray. Sometimes in a solitary place, I spent whole nights in prayer and the Holy Spirit descended. Frequently my mother noticed a light in our bedroom toward midnight, by which she knew that we were still waiting before our Heavenly Father. We had always endeavored in our thoughts, words, and actions to be well-pleasing to the Lord, but now we realized more than ever our own weakness; that we were indeed nothing; and that only in seeking to do God's will, whether in working or resting, whether in peace or peril, in abundance or in want, everywhere and at all times relying on the Holy Spirit, we might accomplish the work the Lord has appointed us to do. If we had good success, we gave all the glory to our Heavenly Father; if bad success, we took all the blame ourselves."

Contrary to what some might think, this man was not some impractical mystic. His day might well include unwearying waiting upon the sick, casting out demons, setting up opium refuges where he ministered to men who, like himself, had been under the power of that drug habit. So real was their devotion, that wife and husband would often set out in different directions that each might make his or her life count more for the distressed, needy souls of China. And so, realizing that much more could be said concerning the devotional life of this unusual convert, we pass on reluctantly.

Jonathan Goforth

Now let us consider the prayerful Jonathan Goforth, the Canadian Presbyterian missionary to China. He began his Christian life, not with the usual quota of five or ten minutes of prayer, but with the habit of rising early each morning in order to get time for unbroken Bible study before going to work or school. If one were to study Goforth's Chinese New Testament, printed in 1926, one would find written on the flyleaf the following note: "October 1932, Have read this Chinese New Testament sixty times." And to get time for such Bible study, he continued the habit of early rising and watched every opportunity, holding the open Bible ready for those odd fragments of time which might be available to him throughout the day. Friends witnessed that Goforth would uncover his head, bowing for a few minutes of prayer before beginning to read the Word of God. This was the secret of his life.

After thirteen years of barren (?) missionary effort Goforth set himself to much more prayer and Bible study. He experienced great heart-searchings as he read of revivals under Finney. Feeling his need of an empowering for service, he sought it hoping to experience the same overwhelming feeling which both Finney and Moody had felt. But his came to him by faith with little feeling other than the peace which accompanies such an indwelling. Following an intensive course of communion, he went forth to experience revival in Manchuria.

When he once wrote to Hudson Taylor asking counsel regarding the entering of a certain province in China, Hudson Taylor replied, "Brother, if you would enter that Province, you must go forward on your knees." This prayer warrior and saint did "go forward" and "on his knees."

Dr. Goforth's book, *By My Spirit,* records the amazing facts of the revival in Manchuria. All but two chapters, the first and the last, were dictated to Fred, his son, as Goforth paced the floor with his hand to his mouth, suffering intense pain from a severe toothache. He wrote the other two chapters later. The following excerpt is both inspiring and challenging:

"The Sword of the Spirit, which is the Word of God, is the only weapon which has ever been mightily used in revival. Where it has been given for what it claims to be, the Word of God has always been like a sharp, two-edged sword, like fire, and like a hammer that breaketh the rock in pieces. When Luther got the Scriptures translated into German, that country was lost to Rome. Moody did not possess the learning of the schools, but he did know his Bible; and it is certain that the world never has known, and doubtful if it ever will know, his equal as an apostle of souls.

"During my student days in Toronto my one weapon, in the jails and slums, was the Bible. In China I have often given from thirty-five to forty addresses in a week, practically all of them being simple Bible rehearsals. In fact, I think I can safely say that, during the forty-one years that I have been on the foreign field, I have never once addressed a Chinese audience without an open Bible in my hand, from which I could say, 'Thus saith the Lord!' I have always taken it for granted that the simple preaching of the Word would bring men to Christ. It has never failed me yet.

"My deepest regret, on reaching three-score years and ten, is that I have not devoted more time to the study of the Bible. Still, in less than nineteen years I have gone through the New Testament in Chinese fifty-five times. That prince of Bible-teachers, Dr. Campbell Morgan, has declared that he would not attempt to teach any book in the Bible unless he had first read it over at least fifty times. Some years ago, I understand, a gentleman attended the English Keswick, and was so fired with a zeal for the Bible that in three years he had read it through twelve times. One would imagine, of course, that he belonged to the leisured class. On the contrary, however, he began his day's work at the Motherwell steel plant at 5:30 a.m.

"During the late Manchu dynasty, scholars were expected to know the classics of their sages off by heart. How do the scholars of so-called Christian lands measure up to that standard as regards the 'World's Great Classic?' It is nothing short of pathetic how so many, who come professedly to represent the Lord Jesus Christ in China, know so little of His Word. Thirty years ago the missionary ideal was to know the Bible so well that one would not have to carry around a concordance. Is the indifference to the Bible today on the part of so many missionaries due to the fact, perhaps, that they have discovered some better means with which to meet the needs of a sin-sick world?"

Goforth tells us in the following paragraphs of hidden intercessors behind the scenes, and of God's power at work:

"When I came to England I met a certain saint of God. She has many bodily infirmities, but her soul is in touch with the living God. We talked about the revival in China and she gave me certain dates when God, in a special manner, pressed her to pray. I was almost startled when I looked up the dates. These were the dates when God was doing His mightiest work in Manchuria and China. There was that saint of God in touch with God's work right through the globe.

"I believe the day will come when the whole inward history of that revival in Manchuria, Korea, and China will be unveiled, showing the one who has done most to bring it about; not the one who speaks to you now, but some of God's saints hidden away secretly with Him in prayer. At one place we had ten wonderful days, when it seemed as if we might ask anything from God and get it. It didn't seem impossible, but the most reasonable thing in the world, to ask on behalf of the hardest cases; and to see them, in a few hours, all broken down on the platform getting rid of hindering sin.

"I could give you case after case from out-station after out-station, places absolutely hopeless because they were so much under the domination of Satan; yet when God came and revived us with united prayer, all the barriers were swept away, and He was magnified....

"At Huang Haien we had one of the wonderful manifestations of Divine power. It was in some respects different from anything I have ever seen. It came over the audience as mysterious as the wind; but it was equal in power to the best I ever saw in Manchuria or elsewhere. After it started it went on for two hours and twenty minutes. I tried to check the frequent bursts of song, but I might as well have tried to check the waves of the sea. Awe and penitence, joy and thanksgiving, and intercession seemed to have no limits. The Lord had visited His people with the Dayspring from on high. They were as if intoxicated. It was splendid order amid perfect disorder. I have never known intercession to have so mighty and wide a sweep before. The people all met again at 3 o'clock next morning, and prayed until daylight."

John Sung

John Sung, a Chinese national, became a widely used minister and evangelist. His secret, too, lay in his evident familiarity with God's Word, and his habitual retiring for communion.

Although a theological student of brilliant capacity, as a result of a combination of overstrain in studying, the emotional disturbance of a friendship, and the assault to his faith regarding the authenticity of the Scriptures, Sung came to the end of himself. One night while praying, the Holy Spirit revealed to him his sin, but also filled his empty, dissatisfied soul with Himself. So overjoyed was this student that he went out into the dormitory halls at midnight praising God for the deliverance wrought.

As a result of these demonstrations, Sung was considered overwrought and mentally disturbed and he found that his Arabia was not a desert but a mental institution! Here, however, the young man whose head had been filled hitherto with theology now had ample time to study the Bible, which he did, reading it through forty times. He used a different plan of systematic study each time, and "was shown a key to the understanding of every one of the 1,189 chapters." He was being trained for future service where for fifteen years he was to influence his own countrymen tremendously. The day he was discharged from the mental hospital he considered to be the day of which he received his highest degree. He had been placed in this institution just seven days after having received his infilling of the Spirit, and unenlightened tutors and staff could not understand the life-giving currents of the Spirit, for doubtless God had given His future servant a further course in Bible study, shot through with the fire of the Holy Ghost.

The fiery evangelist was to beget souls in his likeness. One convert wrote: "Without difficulty I rise very early in the morning to read my Bible and to pray. Otherwise I was very lazy, but now I rise at five o'clock. The Lord changed me into a new creature.... I thank Him out of the deepest of my heart that He sent His servant to us. Now for me it is impossible to be silent. I simply have to give my testimony to everybody."

Nearing the end, as John Sung's body grew weaker and he could not be so active, he still kept up his daily routine of reading eleven chapters of the Bible as well as "earnest, exhausting prayer." Pictures of his spiritual children were before him, and for them he interceded. When a new convert, in his zeal and enthusiasm for Christ, he had burned the theological books, as "books of demons," and transferred his loyalties to the Word of God, so in later life he retained these loyalties up to the end. His fierce denunciations were for those who had departed from the inspired Word and turned to doctrines and traditions of men.

His biographer says: "However late Dr. Sung was kept up at night dealing with correspondence, he was always up at 4:00 or 5:00 a.m. to spend hours on his knees reading his Bible and praying. One man remarking upon John Sung said: 'He talked least, preached more and prayed most.' Everywhere John Sung went he laid emphasis on the urgent need to pray. He could never waste a minute. Revival, he felt, depended upon the prayers that preceded him rather than the preacher."

John Sung had a dying message for the Church today. "The work of the future is to be the work of prayer," he gasped. How prophetic he was, the Church of today will witness. Her weakness, her reliance upon education and brash organization, her fleshly mimicry of worldly methods—all show her depleted strength and departed glory. Prayer will bring the Church back as nothing else will, for a praying Church is a repentant Church and an obedient Church. "The work of the future is to be the work of prayer."

Griffith John

The work of prayer is a hidden work for the most part, and the results are largely invisible. Dr. Griffith John, who spent fifty years of his life as a missionary in China, saw the value of such invisible results and he has left on record his views on the subject:

"The invisible results are, I verily believe, far greater and far more important than the visible. The growth of our work is similar to that of a plant. The root of a plant takes a longer time to grow than the stem; but maturation takes more time than either. The giant oak is wrapped up in that tiny acorn; but to develop it, the acorn must have time to strike its roots, and the sapling must be exposed to the necessary influences. Summer and winter, spring and autumn, the stormy winds and soft breezes have all had a share in, and were all necessary to, the development of the baby oak into the fair tree you see today. So it is with our work. All great work requires time.

"In looking back upon my missionary life, I can see clearly that I have committed many blunders, and that the principal cause was my hurry and bustle. I have had many an illustration in China of the old proverb, 'The greater haste, the less speed.' I would say, Let us beware of allowing ourselves to be driven on by the cry for results. God takes time to accomplish His grand purposes; let us do the same. There was a time when we thought the work of creation was completed in six ordinary days. Geology has taught us a different lesson. Slowly, very slowly, did God build up this wondrous fabric; but see the amount of work that He has put into it. Slowly, very slowly, is He now carrying on a still more glorious work in the moral world; but the foundation has been laid, the superstructure is advancing, in due time the temple will be finished, and again it shall be recorded, 'And God saw everything that He had made, and, behold, it was very good.'

"I don't say that all our converts are genuine; neither do I say that all that are genuine are all that we could wish them to be. But I do mean to say that we have genuine Christians there, and that they have risen rather than fallen, in my estimation since I have had an opportunity of comparing them with the professing Christians of this country."

Chapter Nine

CHINA INLAND MISSION

Hudson Taylor

"There is no way that Christians, in a private capacity, can do so much to promote the work of God and advance the Kingdom of Christ as by prayer," said Jonathan Edwards. Happy and to be envied is that young person who has praying parents, praying friends, and praying companions. Hudson Taylor was particularly blessed of God in this respect, for his early memories were of a father who took his children up to the bedroom to pray and of kneeling at the old bedstead while he poured out his heart in prayer to God for them. Their father's faith in the Bible early instilled a respect for God's Word into Hudson's life which later was to mark the founder of the C.I.M. throughout his leadership of that group in China.

Hudson Taylor's mother likewise, although a very busy woman, found time in the middle of the day to go up to her bedroom and, shutting the door on all the pressing household cares, she poured out her heart for her children, and for their servants and apprentices. God was taking the pains to shape and mold a man of prayer.

Just newly on the field, his letters home reveal the place prayer had in his life: "Oh for more stability! The reading of the Word and meditation upon the promises have been increasingly precious to me of late. At first I allowed my desires to acquire the language speedily to have undue prominence and a deadening effect on my soul. You see from this how much I need your prayers.... The sweetest duties of the day are those that lead to Jesus—prayer, reading, and meditation upon His precious Word."

"One cannot but be impressed," wrote his biographer, "in reading the letters of this period, with the sacred ambition of Hudson Taylor's prayers; a subject worth pondering, if it be true that prayer molds the life and not circumstances, and that as are our deepest desires before God so will the trend of our outward experiences be. Certainly nothing is more significant in this life before us than the longing for usefulness and likeness to the Lord he loved."

And to this good man, God brought a truly good woman who became a real helpmeet in her wifely counsel and prayer. One who knew the family well during these years wrote: "It often comforts me about the children to remember how much she prayed for them. I have seen her at night, when she thought all were sleeping, with head bowed, kneeling for a long, long time on the bare floor. And when I picture her so, I always feel that she was praying most especially for you and the dear children."

And so the leader, Hudson Taylor, grew from an apprenticeship in prayer to be a master at the trade. Someone has said that no sunrise in China found him in bed, in spite of long hours of exhausting labor. And in order to secure quiet for this exalted work, he would sometimes rise in the middle of the night to spend an hour or two undisturbed with God. He instituted days of fasting and prayer when special problems rose to defy the entire group of missionaries, and one testified that never did these days of fasting and prayer fail to meet their need.

As a more mature laborer he writes: "Oh, that we may be made capable of bearing much blessing! Do pray that we may each be drawn close to the Savior, and kept walking with Him in such sweet fellowship that for us to live may be Christ. Then, what wonders would we see! The destitution in the light of eternity is awful. It stares us in the face. Human effort cannot meet it; nothing can, short of divine power. So do pray. Oh! we need to lay hold upon God about it. May He make us really in earnest. How can we trifle, how can we be listless in view of His unfailing promise that what we ask in faith we shall receive? Why are we not Israels? God grant that we may learn how to pray.

"God Himself is the great source of power. Power belongeth unto God.... Further, God's power is available power. We are supernatural people, born again by a supernatural birth, kept by a supernatural power, sustained on supernatural food, taught by a supernatural Teacher from a supernatural Book. We are led by a supernatural Captain in right paths to assured victories...."

While riding on a train with a friend, Hudson Taylor lay back with closed eyes. His friend congratulated him on his having had a refreshing nap but was told by the Director that he had been going over each fellow-missionary by name. Those who spend time with God in the morning will set the tone for praying all day in the busy ways of men.

"It is not lost time to wait upon God," Hudson Taylor comments. "May I refer to a small gathering of about a dozen men in which I was permitted to take part some years ago, in November 1886. We in the China Inland Mission were feeling greatly the need of Divine guidance in the matter of reinforcement, and we came together before our Conference to spend eight days in united waiting upon God, four alternate days being days of fasting as well as prayer. This was November 1886 when we gathered together; we were led to pray for a hundred missionaries to be sent out by our English Board in the year 1887, from January to December. And, further than this, our income had not been elastic for some years; it had been about £22,000; and we had, in connection with that Forward Movement, to ask God for £10,000."

He then told the sequel. The whole number of workers was sent out and a total of £11,000 was received in eleven large gifts! Such believing prayer is surely the greatest gift of God.

"Wonderful thought," wrote this godly leader, "that God should desire fellowship with us! And that He Whose love once made Him the Man of sorrows may now be made the Man of joys by the loving devotion of human hearts! Nothing humbles the soul like sacred and intimate communion with the Lord."

D. E. Hoste

Just as God had honored pleading Moses with a praying Joshua as a successor, so God honored Hudson Taylor with a praying successor in D. E. Hoste. Hoste has this to say about his predecessor:

"He was of necessity a busy man, but he always regarded prayer itself as in reality the most needful and important part of the work. He practically recognized that much time must be spent in seeking God's guidance, if a right understanding was to be obtained of the problems and difficulties that confronted him in carrying on the work of the Mission.

He knew that in no other way was the power of the Holy Spirit to be obtained for himself and his brethren, as they sought to develop the work. I venture on this occasion not only to impress upon myself, but upon you as well, the importance of our copying him in this respect."

D. E. Hoste felt he could unburden his heart and seek advice on the subject of prayer with one who had become a Master-Pray-er. Writing to Hudson Taylor he spoke about the difficulties he found in serving his apprenticeship in prayer:

"I want to ask your prayer and advice as to what is to me a great source of distress and perplexity in my inner life. I find that in prayer wandering thoughts come in, and then in confessing them, often more wandering thoughts come, and in this way often quite a considerable time will be taken up in a desperate struggle to get clear of the various thoughts, and fix the heart and mind in an unwavering concentration on God. You can understand how exhausting this is for one's head; and really now by the time one has been able to pray believingly for them all, one's head is often throbbing, and one is quite wearied. When I see how many are, owing to the neglect of private prayer, gross and heavy and more or less blind, I dare not give it up." Later he writes: "Regarding a wandering mind in prayer, I have found more help in praying aloud, and praying while walking about—talking as to a present Lord—than in any other way."

When he was appointed by Hudson Taylor as Acting General Director of the Mission, the Council expressed its gladness about the appointment, saying: "We needed a man who could give time to prayer, and thus to get to know the mind of the Lord. I am most thankful that you have been led to select, it may be, the most prayerful man among us."

And Phyllis Thompson, his biographer, said: "It was because of his prayerfulness, more than any other quality, that he gained and maintained the confidence of the members of the Mission throughout his thirty-five years' directorship."

Hoste considered prevailing and importunate prayer to be vital in carrying out the work of God. He said: "It is a fact that our minds cannot receive correct impressions of God's plan and methods for the carrying on of the work unless much time is given to waiting upon

Him. Nor will there be spiritual power in our public ministry for the conversion of souls and the real feeding of the flock of God without prolonged and strenuous supplications.

"I remember being early impressed by our Lord's teaching that it would not be easy to obtain the right words, whether for a number or for an individual, whether Christian or pagan. 'I tell you,' He said, 'he will not give him because he is his friend (ye are My friends if you do whatsoever I command you), but because he wearied him.' How much do we know of prevailing importunity for bread with which to feed others? He is no respecter of persons: it is the one who recognizes the true nature of his vocation as a worker for Christ and gives himself to importunate prayer for bread with which to feed others, whether fellow workers, church members, or unbelievers, who will be useful. How often have I for days waited in earnest prayer for right words in replying to a letter dealing with some trouble or difficulty in a district or station. 'If any man speak let him speak as the oracles of God.' 'It is not in me; God shall give Pharaoh an answer of peace,' said Joseph of old. That was not a pose or polite phrase, but a simple, fundamental fact."

So much did D. E. Hoste appreciate the habit of prayerfulness that he thought it should be introduced into the curriculum: "In connection with the Training Home, the thought sometimes comes to me in view of the growing emphasis on prayer and intercession in those parts of the field where there has been special spiritual blessing, whether the exercise of them should not have a more definite and larger place in the course of preparation. The leadership would need to be by someone who, through much exercise, and even travail, has himself been baptized with a true and fervent spirit of prayer.

"Should it not be recognized that the practice of prayer and intercession needs to be taught to young believers, or rather developed in young believers, quite as much, if not more so, than other branches of the curriculum? Unless, however, we ourselves are, through constant persevering practice, truly alive unto God in this holy warfare, we shall be ineffective in influencing others. I am quite sure the rule holds that the more we pray the more we want to pray; the converse also being true."

In order to get time for more prayer, this busy man said: "I find it a good thing to fast. I do not lay down rules for anyone in this matter, but I know it has been a good thing for me to go without meals to get time for prayer. So many say they have not sufficient time to pray. We think nothing of spending an hour or two in taking our meals. It is worth while trying out doing without sometimes. What a benefit it is spiritually, and I believe our digestions would benefit also!

"I find the need of daily spending much time in secret communion with the Lord, if my senses are to be exercised either to discern the state of my brethren or to minister the word in season to them. . . . Is the need of waiting upon God for messages given a sufficient place in our teachings of others? How true it is that the Lord is no respecter of persons."

And regarding the old excuse that we cannot find time for prayer, D. E. Hoste advises: "It is commonplace to say that prayer and secret devotion are important; too often, however, we virtually contradict the words by adding that it is impossible to find time for them. This simply means that, as a matter of fact, we do not regard them as of the first importance. As a rule, we allow at least an hour and a half in the day for the nourishment of our bodies. Why should we expect our Christian life to be strong and helpful to others, if less time is given to secret devotions?" (Selections from the biography of D. E. Hoste by Phyllis Thompson used by permission of the Overseas Missionary Fellowship).

J. O. Sanders

J. O. Sanders, Director of the Overseas Missionary Fellowship, formerly the China Inland Mission, placed a great premium on prayer for their foreign mission efforts. Hudson Taylor had planted the C.I.M. in China through prayer; D. E. Hoste had carried it on as his successor as a man of prayer, and now we hear from one of the more recent directors again emphasizing the dependence they had on the prayers of God's people:

"Our Lord placed the missionary enterprise on a prayer basis when He said, 'Pray ye therefore the Lord of the harvest, that he will send forth laborers into his harvest' (Matt. 9:38). He thus linked us with Himself in the task of getting the Gospel out into the world.

"Prayer is not a desirable addendum to missionary work. It is fundamental, not supplementary to it. If our prayer is meager, it is because we consider it merely supplementary. Barnabas and Saul, the first missionaries, were called in the place of prayer and sent out to the accompaniment of prayer. Ever since that time, the cause of missions has advanced on its knees. There has never been a significant outpouring of the Spirit of God without the previous outpouring of the human spirit to God. All progress can be clearly traced back to prevailing prayer.

"In His sovereignty, God has voluntarily bound Himself to human cooperation in the government of the world. In the spiritual realm, He has also bound Himself to the prayer of faith of His children. This is deeply mysterious but clearly revealed. He links His working with man's praying, and this lays on us a great responsibility. He commands us to pray, and leads us to believe that our prayers can significantly alter the course of events." (From *The Strategic Place of Prayer* by J. Oswald Sanders. Used by permission of the Overseas Missionary Fellowship).

Isobel Kuhn

Isobel Kuhn, whose books have been widely read, was called of God to work among the Lisu tribe. She came to know the Lord in a deep way as these truths we pass on to you will illustrate:

"'And when they had opened their treasures, they presented unto him gifts; gold, and frankincense, and myrrh' (Matt. 2:11)—gold representing our wealth, our possessions we may offer to our King: frankincense as a type of our worship; but the myrrh? That bitter thing? Surely that can only have one meaning. . . the things we are willing to suffer for His sake. . . .

"'Lord, I bring Thee my myrrh.' That was the silent heart-cry that had taken the hurt and fear out of my missionary journey to Lisu-land. I had seldom before been able to offer Him that gift, and I have never forgotten the joy of it.

"There are those who think they are willing to suffer and die 'for Christ's sake,' but who are unwilling to spend half an hour daily in prayer for His work and workers. It is 'myrrh' when we say quietly to friends: 'No, I cannot accept your invitations. I have something I must do,' and then to spend that time in intercession for His work and workers or in some other self-effacing work or drudgery that makes possible the giving of the Gospel to every creature.

"We know a retired schoolteacher who decided to become an 'Intercessory Foreign Missionary.' She listed seventeen missionaries as her own special responsibility and put into this work for Christ all the unselfish heart interest and thoughtfulness that a worldly person puts into making money. She writes to the missionaries and they write to her. She marks down all data about them, their work, their problems and needs, and she bears these as an 'Intercessory Foreign Missionary' to God in prayer. The cost of such giving up of her ease is monotony and obscurity, but it is brought to Him as her 'myrrh' and a life is made exquisitely beautiful by the selflessness of its devotions, made so by the power of the Cross of Christ."

> Make me an Intercessor,
> > Willing for deeper death,
> > Emptied, broken, then made anew,
> > And filled with Living Breath.
>
> Make me an Intercessor,
> > Hidden—unknown—set apart,
> > Thought little of by those around,
> > But satisfying Thine heart.
> > > —Unknown.

Arthur Mathews

Mr. and Mrs. Arthur Mathews spent four years in house arrest on the Tibetan border subsequent to the Communist takeover in 1949. The Mathews, along with their daughter, Lilah, were among the last of the C.I.M. missionaries to leave China. They spent four gruelling years in the school of suffering, but out of it came some profound lessons on prayer which could be learned nowhere else. We quote from *Born for Battle* by Arthur Mathews:

"There were many blunt-edged, self-centered, subjective prayers hammering at Heaven's door clamoring for answers. But God was teaching us, and no school can compare with God's school of hard knocks. Mostly our prayers were stimulated by our fears and the desperate desire to escape from the hands of the communists. From our little corner on the periphery of things we were distracted by the tension of our circumstances and the pressures of duress, to say nothing of the accusations that were being cooked up against us by hate-filled men. Because of all this, our praying focused on our fears, our empty cupboard, and our uncertain future. And while this is the natural impulse, that does not make it the will of God for our praying.

"Our constant struggle was to pull God over to our corner of things until we learned that self-preoccupation in prayer leads to discouragement and depression and that the more our prayers turned inward on our circumstances, the more they became subject to the law of diminishing returns. We were like the disciples when they were caught in a terrible gale while Jesus lay asleep in the stern of their swamped boat. Their preoccupation spilled over in their frenzied shouts, 'Master, carest Thou not that WE perish?' (emphasis mine). Their only thought was about their predicament and the Master's apparent unconcern. For us there came a day when our prayers changed. Worshiping together one morning, we came to see that the story of the storm and the sleeping Savior had a lesson for us on the availability of personal faith for the emergencies of life and that there was really no need to disturb the Lord with our troubles. So as we went to prayer we said, 'Sleep on Lord, for we are not going to waken You.'

"However, after a year or more of other strains, and realizing that nearly all the other missionaries were out of China, we lost our recklessness, and fear began to pile up again. In this predicament God taught us to pray in the spirit of the prayer of the Son, '"I delight to do Thy will, O my God," and since You have placed us here in Communist China for some good and acceptable purpose of Yours, we joyfully abandon ourselves to stay on here as long as You need us here.' We found our strength not in dreams of escape, but in complete surrender to whatever God wanted to do with us, realizing that God's claims are absolute and that we must accept them without bargaining. When God seems to come into our lives like a sword-blade, it is only that He might separate us from ourselves and draw us to Himself.

"The thunderclouds that we had dreaded so much were suddenly transformed into sweet blessing. Like John Bunyan, we almost wanted to pray for greater troubles because of the greater joy they brought in God's assurances. At last our praying had ceased to be an egocentric quest for personal deliverance from trouble and had become a Theocentric tryst that sought first and only, 'Thy will be done on earth as it is in heaven.' We ceased trying to relate God to our problems because we wanted to relate ourselves totally to God's purposes, opportunities, and victory." (Used by Permission of the Overseas Missionary Fellowship).

Chapter Ten

MISSIONARIES IN JAPAN

In this chapter, we are not able by any means to thoroughly cover the whole spectrum of marvelous Japanese missionaries or native evangelists whose sacrificial work is worthy of mention. The oversight is not intentional, but merely because, as the writer to the Hebrews said, "and what shall I say more? For time would fail me to tell. . . ." He had listed some of the more well-known patriarchs, but he knew there were those of the judges and the prophets, not to say anything of a host of individuals, who had never "bowed the knee to Baal," who also deserved mention in this noteworthy chapter.

And what shall we say of the list of somewhat obscure native Christians who, in Japan, endured by faith and triumphed over flood, flame, banishment, torture, and temptation? Then we would not fail to mention the admirable work and fruitfulness of the Cowmans of the Oriental Mission in that land, a work which can never be truly assessed until the Judgment. They sowed the seed faithfully through peril, toil, and pain.

In this chapter, however, we choose to present some prayer warriors from among the pioneer missionaries of the Japanese Evangelistic Band (J.E.B.), having studied their biographies more thoroughly.

Barclay Buxton of the J. E. B.

The work of this devoted Church of England Christian, Barclay Buxton, has ever been a blessing to us. He pioneered the way for others who were to join him in the work which produced some very excellent results in the lives of some Japanese young men. The secret of his devotion will not be hard to discover.

Godfrey Buxton, in a biography about his father, included this outstanding tribute: "Father's gift of opening up the Scriptures had a great influence on us, because behind it were vital secrets in his life. My father died at the age of eighty-five, but I never saw him not fully dressed in the early morning in order to meet the Lord over an open Bible and in prayer. I am sure that he never presumed to feel that 'anything was good enough for us,' even though he had the best of wine of many a convention to give. I am certain that he had prayed over each verse of our Bible study before he passed it on to us. So it had no smack of religious affectation about it, but was life and reality to us boys."

This Christian gentleman placed a very high estimate on the value of prayer previous to conventions which were held in Japan. The workers would come beforehand and would engage in prayer, sometimes long into the night, and then rise early in the morning to follow up their previous effort. Once in Osaka when they met, the Spirit convicted them that they had used means that were fleshly instead of spiritual in their labors, "going down into Egypt for help" and relying on man. It was little wonder that they had times of profound conviction and the presence of the Holy Spirit was enabled to work equipping them for better service upon their return to their fields.

When Barclay Buxton was due to return to England on furlough, he wrote a letter to his fellow-workers in Japan, giving them counsel for maintaining a sturdy Christian life. We quote only part of the letter:

"Do you rise early? None of us ought to be in bed after six, so that we may have at least one quiet hour with God for prayer and reading of His Word before we meet others, and the day's work begins. At special times we must get more—but no Christian can afford to take less than that.

"I advise you as far as possible to fix your times and how you will spend each day. If you do not plan out your time beforehand and keep to your plan, you will often fritter away your time in things that may be good, but are not the best work that you can do. But I specially ask you to fix your times of prayer and let nothing interfere with them. . . .

"Make notes of all you read. Mark the books you read. Have an interleaved Bible in which you can write down any helpful thoughts you receive; and freely write in it. Collect anecdotes, for a good anecdote is worth more than a jewel to you. Keep a book specially for them.

"At noon let us all have fifteen or twenty minutes' intercession for the whole work and for others. For this write down subjects of intercession and divide them into seven, one for every day of the week.

"In visiting take care to get to the point as quickly as possible.... pray before you leave your house for visiting. Pray as you walk to the house. Pray when you have come back, and praise.... Find out whether they are growing in grace and gaining more light from the Word of God. Do they regularly pray and read the Word? Do they get blessing from it?....

"Between that and the evening meeting I advise you to get your second daily hour for reading the Bible and prayer. If we put this off till bedtime we are often so tired that we cannot really profit by it. Fix the hour and keep it.

"In the evenings there will as a rule be meetings to attend. Even if you are not preaching, go to them and pray. Often the one who prays does better work for the meeting than the one who preaches. If you are to preach, you will have prayed much over it beforehand.

"Go to rest early for the sake of your work on the following day. After a solemn meeting let there be no light talking. You have been dealing with the eternal interests of precious souls. Burden your soul before God for them and then go to rest."

Barclay Buxton had entered into the secrets of the Lord and discovered the meaning of a crucifixion of the self-life with the incoming of those rivers of living water which keep the soul inundated with heavenly watering. He felt that the prayers of such a person would have a higher tone to them than the prayers of those who had not known the complete giving of themselves to the Master of the Harvest. He says, "Those who have received the Holy Ghost have also a joy in prayer that they never had before—and an access to God which makes prayer a real time of communion and fellowship. They can intercede for others and obtain what they ask. They obtain fresh promises by prayer continually. And in prayer they are often again filled with the Spirit, in deeper and deeper measure.

"And they have light on the Word. The Bible is a new book to them through which God speaks and shows hidden depths and treasures of His grace. . . . Day by day they gather manna from Heaven to eat. Morning by morning their ears are opened to hear His Word, as a disciple who sits at His feet."

When Mr. Buxton read his Bible, he sat at a table with pen and notebook in hand expecting to receive fresh light from above, and thus he was ready to put down his findings.

When visiting some of the islands by boat, he was stranded for a week because of storms, and so gave that time to prayer. A reliable helper for the work was needed. Thousands of miles away a young man, Paget Wilkes, was feeling the effects of those prayers. He answered the call and became a loyal associate of Barclay Buxton over a long period of time. Thus two men of like mind were joined together in their labors in Japan. This united effort produced young men of high spiritual quality.

Years ago, when reading Barclay Buxton's biography, we were very impressed with some advice he gave to his fellow-workers. We copied it in our Bible, and today we feel it is a very important caution to those who engage in the salvation of souls:

"Chance partnerships have had a devastating influence on the lives of God's servants. With whom we are 'yoked together,' whether in marriage or in His service, will inevitably affect that which we produce. A man may marry and have children. Had he, however, married another, his children would have had a wholly different train of heredity, of spirit, of training, of contacts and possibly emphasis in doctrine and sphere of service. The Holy Spirit teaches us much along this line through the Bible. If such things are true in human relationships, they are also true in the out-workings which result from the partnership of men and women, of varying gifts and personalities, in the work of the Lord. The more that we see how far-reaching are these influences, the more we will take trouble to see that each one brought into a work has been the choice and gift of the ascended Lord for 'the perfecting of the saints, for the work of the ministry, for the edifying of the Body of Christ, till we all come unto the measure of the stature of the fulness of Christ.'" (Selections from *The Reward of Faith in the Life of Barclay Buxton* by Godfrey Buxton are used by permission of Lutterworth Press).

Paget Wilkes

Paget Wilkes, while in Cambridge, received a deep anointing of the Holy Spirit in his life, and later felt the call to go out to Japan as a missionary. His diary readings show also that he was a man who depended upon prayer. "I cry continually to God for fruit that will abide forever. How awful to labor and have nothing that shall abide the searching test that must come to all our service!"

Knowing the great benefit of having prayer partners he wrote asking for prayer:

"The need of all is prayer,

"The second need is prayer,

"The third need is prayer.

"And he himself was above all else a man of prayer. Memory takes one back to the great man of old who, when approached by friends on the subject of a memorial that was to be raised to him after his death, in the form of a statue, said: 'Make it kneeling, for so I came to Glory.'"

Once, when crossing over to Ireland, Wilkes wrote: "Friendship, one is realizing, is only of worth when it is one of prayer. Other friendship, if such a thing can be called friendship, fades away with the fashion of this world, but 'he that doeth the will of God abideth for ever.'"

Later when health was not as robust as when he first began, he gave himself even more to continuous, persevering prayer than previously. "I long to be able to get souls saved and sanctified by prayer alone," he said once to a friend, "without the use of human voice." The following poem is from his own pen:

> Within the veil, there is a secret place
>   Where Christ hath gone to evermore abide,
> And there to plead before His Father's face,
>   The wound-prints of His hands and feet and side.

> It is not strange, though 'tis a grace indeed,
> > That He should ever live to save His own
> Unto the uttermost, and intercede
> > For all the blood-bought jewels of His crown.
>
> But 'tis amazing grace that He should bid
> > Me enter there, and suffer me to dwell,
> Before His Father's presence unafraid
> > And with Him intercede within the veil.

"Intensity in prayer leaves us spent. But it is not safe to relax," he observed, after seeing a soul brought through to Christ.

Those who intercede know something of conflict in prayer as did Paget Wilkes. "Let us remember that these souls, out here and everywhere, are surrounded by 'wicked spirits' in heavenly places and so our fight and your fight is the same—'Prayer.' 'Praying' is generally pronounced 'playing' by English-speaking Japanese, because they cannot get a clear distinction between 'R' and 'L', but though the pronunciation is the same, the doing of it is not! Praying out here is undoubtedly not playing, though the devil does his best to make us think so.

"A thought that has been a great blessing lately is II Tim. 2:25-26, where we are bidden to instruct with all meekness the unsaved, or backsliders, yea, and cold Christians too, for that matter. That is to say, when we meet with some exceptionally difficult, irritating and hopelessly conceited soul, how easy to see the man and put down to his account all his sin and folly. But the Lord bids us put it down to the devil, to the devil's trap and the devil's captivity. The man is to be pitied as a captive. If we lay hold of this by the Spirit of God, it will be easier to love the unlovable sinner. If we look beyond and below the sinner, and see all the hideous power of evil and Satan taking the man captive at his will, it will be easy to love with compassion, as the Lord loved us, yea, and still loves them. We poor, saved sinners have but to discern the spirits of evil, and war with them, by faith, and prayer and love, seeking their deliverance from the captivity of which they are ignorant."

After Paget Wilkes had once prayed, while in England, for a mental sufferer, on whose behalf a half night of prayer was spent, the Lord laid the burden of Japan upon the heart of this lady's friend, Mrs. Wood, because she felt Mr. Wilkes had been enabled "not to seek his own things," but had given himself for the deliverance of her friend. It was during a prayer-meeting that the Lord had laid it on her heart with such assurance that she could not doubt it was from Him. She continued to bear Japan upon her heart before the Throne of Grace.

Kochi San

Paget Wilkes, in his book, *Missionary Joys in Japan,* tells the story of Kochi San whom he had met in his missionary travels:

"I had the pleasure of meeting once more Kochi San, who has spent nearly half his life behind the walls of the great convict prison in the Hokkaido. Committing murder when about nineteen, he was condemned to death; and while waiting his execution (he could not read at the time) he heard, for the first time, from a Christian warder those life-giving words, 'I am the Resurrection and the Life; he that believeth on me, though he were dead, yet shall he live.' But, alas! As soon as his sentence was commuted to penal servitude for life—twenty-five years—his good impressions passed away as a morning cloud.

"It was not till eight years later that he was again convicted of sin, and that without any human agency. At the same time, through a dream in which an angel appeared to him with the Bible, saying, 'Take and read,' he learned to read and once more turned to the Word of God. Powerfully converted, he committed the whole of the New Testament to memory during the remaining seventeen years of imprisonment. He was at once used of the Lord in bringing the message of salvation to his fellow-prisoners; but though he never once lost his assurance of salvation, and was instrumental in leading men to Christ, he soon began to discover the remains of sin in his nature. The words, 'Love thinketh no evil' and 'Love never faileth' were like a sharp sword in his bones, revealing both what he was and, by the grace of God, what he might and ought to be.

"Without any teaching from man on the possibility, need, and way of entire sanctification in this life, he was taught of the Lord that Christ died to cleanse us from all sin, inward and outward, and that the Holy Ghost was able to fill us with perfect love. For four years he struggled with his evil nature—fasting, praying, and repenting amain; till, in despair, after some hours of fasting in the intense heat, during which time he was mercilessly tormented with mosquitoes, he told us how, like a flash of lightning, God revealed to him the power of the precious blood to cleanse him from all indwelling sin.

"From that blessed day, persecuted and opposed, tempted and tried, he has never let go his confidence, and never found the Lord to fail, or His precious blood insufficient to keep him clean and sweet and loving. This gave him power to lift up his eyes, like Stephen of old, to behold the Lord standing at the right hand of God, when troubles and oppositions and dangers have been flying like stones about his head. He has proved it true that the love shed abroad in his heart does keep him from thinking evil, even of his persecutors, and that it never faileth. He is traveling everywhere, in town and village, unattached to any mission, trusting only God for his supplies, and finding an abundant entrance into unopened places, where he proclaims a full salvation for the vilest sinner. God seals his service in no ordinary degree, for He has found in him a man utterly devoted to both sinner and Savior." (Used by permission of Marshall, Morgan, and Scott).

With apologies to David, the Psalmist, Toki Miyashiro has written a psalm for the person who is confronted with the life of busyness in our Western world.

> The Lord is my pace setter
> I shall not rush.
> He makes me stop,
> And rest for quiet intervals.
>
> He provides me with images of stillness
> Which restore my serenity.

He leads me in ways of efficiency
Through calmness of mind.
And His guidance is peace.

Even though I have a great many things
To accomplish each day,
I will not fret,
For His presence is here,
His timelessness,
His all-importance,
Will keep me in balance.

He prepares refreshment and renewal
In the midst of my activity.
My cup of joyous energy overflows.
Surely harmony and effectiveness
Shall be the fruits of my hours,
For I shall walk in the pace of my Lord,
And dwell in His house for ever.

* ** * * * * * *

A most striking answer to prayer came to a missionary institution in Japan. A missionary records the coming of God into that school:

"Another experience came in the fall of 1882 and the spring of 1883. I found that a spirit of speculation and doubt of many of the vital doctrines of the Gospel had come into the school, and was among some of the pastors as well. The preaching was too much of a speculative, philosophical character. Doubts of the Divinity of Christ and especially of the reality of the Holy Spirit, were rife in our school, even among some of the teachers. I felt a great agony of prayer for this, as did some of my colleagues.

"When the Week of Prayer came, the first of January, it passed without any special result, and we held it over a second week, having a general meeting every evening to pray especially for the outpouring of God's Spirit upon the school. But no result came. Then a little band of perhaps ten held on praying daily for this object.

"The first part of February I felt prompted to write a letter stating the spiritual condition of the school, and our needs, and asking for special prayer for the outpouring of God's Spirit upon our school. I made forty copies of it, and sent them to most of our colleges and theological seminaries in the United States. The weeks wore on, and there was no sign here. The little bank of praying ones had decreased to half a dozen. On Sabbath, March 16, 1883, in the afternoon and evening, an invisible influence struck the school. None of the teachers knew of it until the next morning. But of the one hundred and fifty young men then in the school very few closed their eyes in sleep that night. Almost every room was filled with men crying to God for mercy. The professing Christians were at first under the deepest conviction of sin.

"This experience lasted a whole week, during which there was no preaching. The whole movement was to human eye spontaneous and almost the only efforts which the teachers put forth was to restrain from excesses and guide the inquiring souls into the light. All but four or five who were in the school passed through the experience, and the work spread from our school to the churches in this part of Japan, and this revival changed the whole spirit of the school. There have been no doubts since that time of the existence and work of the Holy Spirit.

"About the middle of April, answers to my letters came, and they told us that on March 12-17, and so on, companies were praying for the outpouring of the Spirit upon the Doshisha, some of them saying that they were praying 'with strong crying and tears.'

"Let the date of the prayers in our country and the date of the blessing in another country be compared, and this remarkable answer to prayer cannot but be a great encouragement to others to pray."

Chapter Eleven

MISSIONARIES IN THE ORIENT

Thousands of worthy laborers in God's harvest field have toiled on unnoticed and unknown. Some have kept diaries so that their inmost thoughts and struggles were detailed. Here they gave insight into their life of communion with God. Others wrote letters which later were gathered into a book. Many of these, however, are no longer available for the reader of today. Their laurels and rewards are known on high.

We are again limited both as to time and space to record all that we would like, but we will include several better known ministers and missionaries who went to countries with most forbidding frontiers. There, where previously little toil had been expended by earlier sowers, they planted the Gospel seed.

We cite briefly the cases of two missionaries: One is Adoniram Judson, whose toils, suffering, and losses in property, wives, and children is almost unparalleled in missionary annals.

The other is that of Anthony Norris Groves, the brother-in-law of George Müller of Bristol. He left a lucrative dental practice in England to go out by faith to the Orient. His biography by G. H. Lang gives a most spiritual insight into the life of this man who dared to risk all for Christ.

The Judsons of Burma

First let us hear a message on prayer from the jungles of Burma. The writer is Adoniram Judson. How different was his code of prayer-living from that of many both at home and abroad today who, having spent a stated time in the morning, become absorbed with work and business:

"Secret prayer is commonly considered a duty which must be performed every morning and evening, in order to keep a conscience void of offence. But do not, my dear brother, entertain an opinion as defective. Consider secret prayer as one of the three great works of thy life. Arrange thy affairs, if possible, so that thou canst leisurely devote two or three hours every day, not merely to devotional exercises, but to the very act of secret prayer and communion with God. Endeavor several times a day, to withdraw from business and company, and lift up thy soul to God in private retirement.

"Begin the day by rising after midnight to this sacred work. Let the hour opening dawn find thee at the same work; let the hours of nine, twelve, three, six, and nine at night witness the same. Be resolute in this course. Make all practicable sacrifices to maintain it. Consider that the time is short, and that business and company must not be allowed to rob thee of God. At least, remember the morning, noon, and night season, and the season after midnight, if not detrimental to the health."

It appears that Dr. Judson became intensely interested in behalf of the Jews while he was laboring among the heathen in Burma. He not only prayed earnestly for their conversion but awakened an interest in others also, so that he raised one thousand dollars toward a mission in Palestine.

He urged the Baptist Missionary Union to undertake this work among the Jews, but, to his great regret, the enterprise was not executed. Were his prayers, then, left unanswered? Let the facts speak.

Many years subsequent—indeed, only two weeks before his death—Mrs. Judson read him this extract from Dr. Hague's journal of travels in the East:

"There at Mr. Goodell's house in Constantinople, we first learned the interesting fact, which was mentioned by Mr. Schauffler, that a tract has been published in Germany giving some account of Dr. Judson's labors in Ava; that it had fallen into the hands of some Jews and had been the means of their conversion; that it had reached Trebizond, where a Jew had translated it for the Jews of that place; that it had awakened a deep interest among them; that a candid spirit of inquiry had been manifested; and that a request had been made for a missionary to be sent them from Constantinople."

Mrs. Judson writes:

"His eyes were filled with tears when I had done reading, but still he at first spoke playfully and in a way that a little disappointed me. Then a look of almost unearthly solemnity came over him and, clinging fast to my hand as though to assure himself of being really in the world, he said, 'Love, this frightens me; I do not know what to make of it.'

"'What?'

"'Why, what you have been just reading. I never was deeply interested in any object, I never prayed sincerely and earnestly for anything, but it came; at some time, no matter how distant a day; somehow, in some shape, probably the last I should have desired, it came. And yet I have had so little faith! May God forgive me and, while He condescends to use me as His instrument, wipe the sin of unbelief from my heart.'"

Dr. Adoniram Judson writes from Burmah to a friend in America: "Remember, I pray you, that word of Brainerd: 'Do not think it enough to live at the rate of common Christians. True, they will call you uncharitable and censorious, but what is the opinion of poor worms of the dust that it should deter us from our duty?' Remember that other word of the same holy man, 'Time is but a moment, life a vapor, and all its enjoyments but empty bubbles and fleeting blasts of wind.'" Again Dr. Judson writes, "Let me beg of you not to rest contented with the commonplace religion that is now prevalent."

A. N. Groves

A. N. Groves speaks of prayer as the place of Christian safety. He also shows that the invalid saint can, by prayer, accomplish as much as the most active worker.

"'Wait on thy God CONTINUALLY,' and the beginning of departure is found in only waiting upon God OCCASIONALLY. There is something in the heart which tells us if we are really in fellowship with God; the soul that has tasted it cannot be mocked by an apparent return. One cause of going astray is the preferring something to God's worship, even as Israel followed Baalim. Often we are beguiled into worldly things with an idea that we can make them subservient to God's glory; but the things we have thought would bend, as a bow, to shoot arrows against the enemies of God, become the means of piercing us through with many sorrows, and leading us away from God. Nothing requires more spiritual discernment than to detect the snares of the enemy; they are often so covered over as to appear the leadings of God.

"How consolatory it is to feel that holiness is the only influence in the Church of God worthy the ambition of a child of God, and that

that influence is as much within the reach of a bedridden member of the family as of those who are flourishing in the zenith of their popularity; and that the prayers of the holy bedew the Church with as many blessings as the labors of the active, if prayers are all that the providence and fatherly dispensation of the Most High allow them to offer."

Modern Missionary Standard

As we have seen above, Dr. Judson's daily routine devoted a large percentage of time to prayer. In contrast, the following is a diary extract of a modern missionary which we cut out of a religious periodical some years ago. We have removed the names of places, etc., so as to conceal the identity of the missionary:

"Arise 5:30 a.m. tea ready.

"Write to P___ G___.

"Seventeen tenants request for permission to excavate tank in K___. Visit site: encourage them. Receive objections from rival claimants; promise to investigate.

"Leave for ___ (about 27 miles) on push-bike.

"Call at ___ (17 miles) see our land agent and rent collector.

"Delightful ride through jungle to ___ (10 miles). Arrive in good time.

"Examine village school and tell children a story.

"Rice, provided by ___, the preacher.

"Rest—read Harma's Village (novel in Santali).

"Tea.

"Visit the whole village of ___ inviting all to gramophone recital.

"Return, dusk; gramophone, preaching, and prayers.

"___ brings suggestion for morrow; make program.

"Rice, forget it is my birthday until I discover the special curries.

"___, the teacher, reports all well in the village and discusses the desirability of forming a Young People's Society.

"And so to bed."

Chapter Twelve

EXPERIMENT IN REVIVAL

Some years ago we printed this remarkable incident in our *Message of Victory* magazine. It tells of a missionary in India who made an experiment with prayer which brought about remarkable results. We reprint it here, trusting that it will help us to see the true perspective of prevailing prayer.

Flemming in his book, *The Dynamic of All Prayer,* asks the question, "What part has prayer to play in God's processes and operations? Is it a *secondary* part or is it a *primary* one?" He says that the current view in most circles until quite recently, and the view that is held in many minds until today is this—that the real work of the Church and of Jesus Christ is done in the pulpit and on the platform, in the classroom and by personal influence. This is the *Fundamental* work and prayer comes in as *Supplemental* to it. We believe that much the same view is held by many Christian workers in India. The "work" is so pressing that there is little time for prayer. All readily admit the value of prayer, that it is well (as Flemming says) "to have an introduction to prayer and that all work should be wound up by prayer"; but it must not encroach on the work proper.

We believe that this is putting the emphasis in the wrong place, making prayer a secondary matter when according to the Word of God prayer is the primary work. If we could only give prayer its right place what a change would come over our work in India! Would this really bring about a change? Would it mean more success if we made prayer our primary work and preaching and teaching secondary?

The following account of a lady missionary who has been a faithful member of our Prayer Union for many years, will show us how this has succeeded in her case and we firmly believe there would be similar results in every instance where proper emphasis is placed on prayer.

This worker often sent requests for prayer to our Circular in years gone by and she always deplored the sad state of the work in her district—the hardness of the soil, the lack of fruit, the indifference of the Indian workers, her own lack of passion for souls, etc. She considered her own field the hardest field in India; she was almost in despair at times. These requests were scattered over the years 1910 to 1912.

We believe that the above description is a picture of the conditions of the work in scores of Indian stations.

In July, 1913, we printed in the *Remembrancer* an incident showing how the late Rev. J. N. Hyde gave himself to prayer and with what result; and quoting a letter from Mr. Chapman, the Evangelist, describing the impression that dear Hyde's prayer life made on him.

The lady missionary referred to, read this account and the Holy Spirit so impressed her that she resolved to carry out what she felt the Spirit of God had been prompting her to do for some time, viz., to make intercession her primary work as a missionary. This is how she wrote to us then, and her communication was published in the *Remembrancer* for October, 1913.

"This incident about dear Hyde's prayer life published in the *Remembrancer* has been a great help to me and I believe it will be used to help others. For a long time the Lord has been calling me to a deeper work of intercession, and of late I have felt the call increasingly to give my life more to the ministry of prayer. It has not been easy to yield to this call, for it may mean misunderstanding on the part of my fellow-workers, as it did with Mr. Hyde. Since reading this incident in Mr. Hyde's life, I feel that at any cost I must know and live this prayer life, and so at last the battle of my heart for many months is ended.

"I feel that from this time forth my life work is to be the ministry of intercession. I do not mean to exclude active work; that will come in as I have time for it, but I do feel that this other ministry is to be my real life-work. And how much India needs prayer. It came to me yesterday what a great work even the humblest of us can do by prayer. In our Mission work, the strongest and the most talented even can touch but a small number of people, comparatively, with their influence, but *with our prayers we may each one girdle not only India but the globe.*

"Strange how dense we are that we cannot see this. Why should we place greater value on our own feeble, puny effort than upon reaching up and 'moving the Hand that moves the world?' When we think of such promises as 'Call upon Me, and I *will* answer, and will show thee great and mighty things,' it is a very simple conclusion that the reason we do not see 'great and mighty things' is because we do not 'call.' What else can it be in the face of such a promise? I believe the world has yet to see what can be done by patient, persevering, prevailing prayer."

This letter, when read in connection with her previous requests for prayer, revealed to us two or three things:

(a) That she had labored hard and faithfully for the Master for years, and that without seeing any fruit.

(b) That she was taking up this life of intercession, after a great struggle in obedience to the call of Christ.

(c) That she was afraid of being misunderstood by her fellow-workers.

In less than a year she wrote another letter, and oh! what a change!! The Lord had heard her prayer, and the wilderness was being changed into a fruitful garden. Fifteen were baptized before the end of the year, and one hundred and twenty-five adults during the first half of the following year.

We cannot do better than reproduce her letter:

"It is almost a year ago, I think, since I wrote to you of the definite call I felt from God to give myself more fully to the life of prayer and intercession. It has been in my mind often lately to tell you something of the result of the decision which I made then.

"The most of the year has been a battle to keep to my resolution. There has been no opposition from the other missionaries, for my work is quite separate and only the members of the family in which I live have known this new way into which God has led me and they are most sympathetic. But the opposition has come from within, not without. At first the temptation came—'Suppose you see no immediate result of your prayers. If God should keep you waiting perhaps years for any blessing in your work, if things go on just the same in spite of all the time you give to prayer, can you trust God and pray on until the answer comes? or even if the answer never seems to come?' It was hard, but

God gave grace to feel that I could pray on although I might never see the fruit of it.

"Then came what was even a harder struggle. I have always lived such an active life, accustomed to steady work all the day long, and my new life called for much of the best part of the day to be spent in prayer and Bible study. Can you not imagine what it was? and what it is sometimes now? To hear others going around hard at work, while I stayed quietly in my room as it were inactive.

"Many a time my heart has longed to be out in active work among the people in the rush of life, but God would not let me go. His hand held me with as real a grip as any human hand and I knew that I could not go. This experience often comes to me yet. Only the other day I felt it and then with the old longing God seemed to say, 'what fruit had ye then in those things of which ye are now ashamed?' Ashamed! Yes, I knew I was heartily ashamed of the years of almost prayerless missionary life; I do not know of anything in my past life I am more ashamed of. And what fruit had I? I can look back over eight years in India, eight years of hard work, unceasingly from morning to night, and very, very little fruit of any kind.

"And today? *Not quite a year yet of this new prayer life, yet there are such changes.* You know something through my requests for prayer and praise of the turning towards Christ of the people in the villages. Last year we reported fifteen adult baptisms during the year. This year during the last six months over 125 adults have been baptized and there are still a large number of enquirers. In several villages where a few months ago we had no work whatever, we have now small Christian communities and day schools and the work is spreading. The evangelistic work here in ____ has never been what it is today. I am not specially associated with this movement, in fact, I do not think anyone connects me with it particularly; our senior missionary is the leader in it, and I am more than glad to have it so; there is such a joy, I think, in being a hidden instrument and it is far safer.

"With every department of my work things are in a more prosperous condition than I have ever known them to be; and yet I give but half the time to my work that I once did; still I do not feel that anything is neglected. *The stress and strain have gone out of my life*. I find that I can do my work quietly with none of the feeling of hurry which once characterized it. And the joy of feeling that my life is evenly balanced—the life of work and the life of communion—brings constant rest and peace.

"I could not go back to the old life now—it does not seem as though I could, and God grant that it may always be impossible.

"I have written this just as a testimony to His faithfulness and to the wide-reaching value of the prayer life, and especially of the life of intercession. It is this from which Satan is keeping so many of God's children. Our rightful heritage on earth is the life of communion and how few of us enter into it. I have only touched the border land, and the more I enter into this prayer life the more conscious I am of my weakness in it. The other day a request came to me for prayer. I never had anything humble me more, for it seemed to take me down about as low as I could get in spirit. But it is always a comfort to think how God can use us in our weakness, is it not? 'The weak things of this world, and the base things of this world.' Some of us could not get along without that verse.

"We need much prayer for these new converts, if they are to stand fast in the faith and grow in the knowledge of Christ; but I do not feel that we need to be anxious about them, for 'He is able.'"

With this interesting letter, we received the following requests which breathe of life and spiritual success:

"Much praise for His continued working in the villages. People are sending to us, asking for the Gospel to be preached to them. In the last six months quite a number have been baptized and we have now little Christian communities in several villages where we had no work at all before. Thanks be to Him. Praise for His evident blessing upon other parts of the work. Praise for *Himself,* His hourly presence and fellowship. Pray that these new converts may grow in grace and in the knowledge of Him. Pray that we may know how to lead them on, and that we may be given patience in dealing with them."

We received another letter quite recently showing that the work is growing in interest and power, so that this prosperity is *not a mere flash but a permanent blessing.* This is how she writes: "You will be glad to know that the work here still goes on. The spirit of earnest enquiry is increasing in all the villages and there is every promise of a greater movement in the future than we have yet had. *Our Christians now number 600 in contrast with one-sixth that number two years ago.* I believe we may expect soon to see great things all over India."

"Prayer changes things" is an expression that we have often seen on cards; what we have given is a concrete instance or example of the present day, where prayer has changed the whole working of a mission station and district. One worker, after counting the cost, definitely gave herself to a life of prayer, expecting opposition, ready to continue this life even though she might never see any result. The district was a difficult one; work had been going on with little or no result for years, but when prayer became the *primary* work of this missionary there was almost an immediate change and God continues to work.

Our question to every reader is, What place does prayer have in your life? Has it the first place or a secondary place? We all believe in prayer but is it fundamental work? Or supplemental?

We may think that our work is so urgent that we cannot give time to prayer; but this worker says, and many would confirm her statement, that the work has not suffered in any way; *one is able to do more work, when prayer has its rightful place in our lives;* the work runs more smoothly, difficulties vanish away, when we take everything to the Lord in prayer.

Shall this be a message for you, dear fellow-worker? Let us revise our estimate of the values of spiritual forces. Shall we make prayer our chief work?

We are passing through a critical period, conflict on every side, and when the work is on the eve of tremendous success, we have to face financial difficulties, shortness of funds, reduction of expenses, and possibly of workers. Was there ever a time when we are so urgently called and driven to prayer? The only way to solve these problems is on our knees.

P. S. It is scarcely necessary to add that the letters quoted above were never intended for publication. The lady's permission to make use of them was given on the strict understanding that her name and her mission station should not be mentioned. F. S. E. Used by permission.

Not in the tumult of the rending storm,
    Not in the earthquake or devouring flame,
But in the hush that could all fear transform,
    The still, small whisper to the Prophet came.

O Soul, keep silence on the mount of God,
    Though cares and needs throb round thee like a sea;
From supplications and desires unshod,
    Be still, and hear what God shall say to thee.

O rest, in utter quietude of soul,
    Abandon words, leave prayer and praise awhile,
Let thy whole being, hushed in His control,
    Learn the full meaning of His voice and smile.

—Mary Rowles Jarvis.

Chapter Thirteen

MISSIONARIES IN INDIA

"To arouse one man or woman to the tremendous power of prayer for others is worth more than the combined activity of a score of average Christians. What David Brainerd did, others may do. God is no respecter of persons."

These are the words of A. J. Gordon and how true they are! E. M. Bounds also emphasized prayer above work by personal example. He says: "There must be much of the invisible and the underground growth, or else the life will be feeble and short-lived. . . . To be too busy with God's work to commune with God, to be busy with doing church work without taking time to talk to God about His work, is the highway to backsliding. Many people have walked therein to the hurt of their immortal souls. Notwithstanding great activity, great enthusiasm, and much hurrah for the work, the work and the activity will be but blindness without the cultivation and the maturity of the graces of prayer."

We present other prayer examples—missionaries to that great subcontinent of India. The way they fought off discouragement, combated an unhealthy climate, attacked a hoary system deeply rooted for centuries, and most of all, won many precious souls for the Master, chiefly by prayer, should inspire us all.

From the book, *Apostle of the North,* we find the same sentiments expressed by a Christian worker:

"'What has been the secret of your marvelous success in India?' was asked not long ago of a fair, delicate, young lady missionary, who had been most marvelously owned of God in the conversion of many hundreds of once degraded, benighted Telegus. Her answer is worthy of remembrance of all who are toiling for the advancement of the Kingdom of Christ at home, as well as abroad. Modestly, but in a way that thrilled all who heard her, she replied:

"'I never let my missionary duties, heavy and ma ny though they are, rob me of the time devoted to private devotions and communion with Christ through prayer and His Word. I found it better to limit my time for meals and sleep, rather than the time consecrated to personal communion with God alone. If a sick Hindu came to see me when at prayer, I finished my devotions as usual and ever felt that I was so much the better prepared to prescribe more wisely for the disease; and in this I have never been mistaken.'

"These are words worthy of being pondered over by us all. In these active days there is so much fuss and flutter, and we seem to be so busy amidst the multitudinous duties that come to us. We cannot therefore be too careful in guarding our own soul's interest and the time when we go apart from the world and commune alone with Him Who is the source of our strength."

Henry Martyn

Next we turn to the diary of Henry Martyn. He was but twenty-four years of age when he left Britain to go out to India as a missionary, and we quote diary records of his devotional life when aboard ship en route to the country of his destination:

"My mind, this morning, easily ascended to God in peaceful solemnity. I succeeded in finding access to God, and being alone with Him. Could I but enjoy this life of faith more steadily, how much should I 'grow in grace,' and be renewed in the spirit of my mind. At such seasons of fellowship with the Father and His Son Jesus Christ, when the world, and self, and eternity, are nearly in their right places, not only are my views of duty clear and comprehensive, but the proper motives have a more constraining influence. . . . I came to my rooms rejoicing to be alone again, and to hold communion with God."

"Found great pleasure and profit in *Milner's Church History*. I love to converse, as it were, with those holy bishops and martyrs, with whom I hope, through grace, to spend a happy eternity."

"Read Isaiah the rest of the evening, sometimes happy, but at other times tired, and desiring to take up some other religious book; but I saw it an important duty to check this slighting of the Word of God."

"Endeavored to consider what should be my study and preparation for the mission; but could devise no particular plan, but to search the Scriptures. What are God's promises respecting the spread of the Gospel, and the means by which it shall be accomplished? Long seasons of prayer in behalf of the heathen, I am sure, are necessary. (Isa. 62). Began Isaiah, and learnt by heart the promises scattered through the first twelve chapters hoping that they may prove profitable matter for meditation as well as prayer."

"I am born for God only. Christ is nearer to me than father, or mother, or sister—a nearer relation, a more affectionate Friend; and I rejoice to follow Him and to love Him."

"My whole soul wrestled with God. I knew not how to leave off crying to Him to fulfil His purposes; chiefly pleading His own glorious power. I do not know that anything would be a Heaven to me, but the service of Christ and the enjoyment of His presence. O how sweet is life, when spent in His service! I am going upon a work exactly according to the mind of Christ; and my glorious Lord, Whose power is uncontrollable, can easily open a way for His feeble follower, through the thickest of the ranks of His enemies. And now, on let me go, smiling at my foes; how small are human obstacles, before this mighty Lord! How easy it is for God to effect His purposes in a moment! What are inveterate prejudices, when once the Lord shall set to His hand! In prayer I had a most precious view of Christ, as a Friend that sticketh closer than a brother. Oh, how sweet was it to pray to Him! I hardly knew how to contemplate with praise enough His adorable excellencies. Who can show forth all His praise!"

After arriving in India, his diary records his continued aspirations after God: "How sweet is prayer to my soul at this time. I seem as if I could never be tired, not only of spiritual joys, but of spiritual employments, since these are now the same."

"I felt as if I could never be tired with prayer. . . At night read the third and fourth chapters of the Acts; and lost much time and spirituality by indulging ideas of schemes about the Gospel, which had more of romance and pride in them than of wisdom and humiliation."

While engaged in the translation of the Bible, he shares with us his delights in meditation on this Book: "All day on the translations; employed a good while at night in considering a difficult passage; and being much enlightened respecting it, I went to bed full of astonishment at the wonders of God's Word. Never before did I see anything of the beauty of the language, and the importance of the thoughts, as I do now. I felt happy that I should never be finally separated from the contemplation of them, or of the things concerning which they are written. Knowledge shall vanish away, but it shall be because perfection shall come. Then shall I see as I am seen, and know as I am known."

"What a source of perpetual delight have I in the precious Book of God! O that my heart were more spiritual, to keep pace with my understanding; and that I could feel as I know. May my root and foundation be deep in love, and may I be able to 'comprehend, with all saints, what is the breadth, and length, and depth, and height, and to know the love of Christ which passeth knowledge!' And may I be filled with all the fulness of God! May the Lord, in mercy to my soul, save me from setting up an idol of any sort in His place; as I do by preferring even a work professedly done for Him, to communion with Him. How obstinate is the reluctance of the natural heart to love God! But, O my soul, be not deceived; thy chief work upon earth is to obtain sanctification, and to walk with God. 'To obey is better than sacrifice, and to hearken than the fat of rams.' Let me learn from this that to follow the direct injunctions of God, as to my own soul, is more my duty than to be engaged in other works, under the pretence of doing Him service."

"The determination with which I went to bed last night, of devoting this day to prayer and fasting, I was enabled to put into execution. In my first prayer for deliverance from worldly thoughts, depending on the power and promises of God, for fixing my soul while I prayed, I was helped to enjoy much abstinence from the world for nearly an hour. Then read the history of Abraham, to see how familiarly God had revealed Himself to mortal men of old. Afterward, in prayer for my own sanctification, my soul breathed freely and ardently after the holiness of God, and this was the best season of the day."

Of his native assistant in translating the Bible, he says, "Sabat lives almost without prayer, and this is sufficient to account for all evils that appear in saint or sinner."

William Carey

We used to often wonder at the colossal task undertaken by Carey and his colleagues and marveled at the accomplishments achieved during his lifetime. We discovered the secret through reading a religious paper from India. The unknown author says:

"The secret was that Carey had someone who was available to God to intercede for him. He had an invalid sister, a victim of paralysis, bedridden for fifty years. Most of the time she was unable to speak. But all the time Carey was in India she wrote encouraging letters to him and prayed for him. Where are such saints today? Availability is an attitude of the heart and a matter of obedience to God. It has nothing to do with physical conditions. Will you ask God to deliver you from the things that bind your heart and to set you free so that you can be available to Him to carry His burden?"

***   ***   ***

"'If two of you shall symphonize on earth as touching anything that they shall ask it shall be done for them of my father which is in Heaven.' The word, symphonize, is a musical term," wrote A. T. Pierson, "referring to the harmony of notes in a chord, which is possible only when each accords with the whole instrument. One note, out of tune, will turn accord into discord. So the power of joint supplication depends not on the numbers gathered, but on the measure of real agreement of each with the mind and will of God. One out of accord with Him hinders perfect harmony with the rest; hence the smallest number that can agree is specified, because there is more power when two pray, provided they truly agree, than when a larger number apparently unite but such agreement is lacking. Numbers are of no importance, but perfect harmony is."

In the *Evangelical Christian* many years ago this fascinating story was told: "Some years ago a bedridden lady in Scotland requested of a missionary in India names for her prayer list of any for whose salvation he was laboring. He sent the names of twelve stalwart non-caste Telegus. Hence, up in the highlands of Scotland, this praying partner of the missionary wrestled in constant intercession with the Lord of the harvest.

"They both claimed the promise, 'If two of you shall agree on earth as touching anything that they shall ask, it shall be done for them of my Father which is in heaven' (Matt. 18:19).

"The twelve men were soon under the Spirit's conviction and transforming power, and by the grace of God were changed into men of cleansed heart and life, and of constancy in prayer.

"But for a season these men disappeared for parts unknown to our missionary. The following year he was in the hill country for a brief rest. There he heard of these men from a wealthy Scottish coffee planter of Ceylon. This was his story:

"It was during an epidemic that had swept over the plantations of his district, carrying away many of the workers, and bringing operations almost to a standstill. But one day at noon a knock was heard on his office door. When he opened it, there stood twelve Telegu men whom he had often noticed as always working together in the off-hours. 'Master,' they said, 'we want you to hold a prayer meeting with us. We believe our God will stop this scourge if we come to Him.'

"'All right,' replied the coffee planter, 'come back in ten minutes.'

"Then he locked the door and wrestled with himself. He said, 'These men think I am a Christian, and I'm not. Shall I dismiss them when they return, or shall I let them know what I am and go right ahead with the prayer-meeting, or what shall I do?' After a severe struggle he decided to settle the whole matter right there, and accept Christ into his heart and life, with His pardoning and empowering grace.

"The twelve Telegus arrived promptly at the end of the time specified, the door was opened to them with a welcome and there was a wonderful prayer-meeting in which all, including the operators, took part. On that day and hour, the epidemic ceased. There were no more cases, either for the hospital or for the pyre. And these twelve men of the coffee plantation were the twelve of the prayer list up in Scotland.

Where two agree as prayer-partners, how great and how far the reach of faith."

Sadhu Sundar Singh

The prayer life and efforts of Sadhu Sundar Singh reveal the secret of his life-accomplishments. Here we find an Indian holy man, wonderfully saved. Having practiced austerities and devotions of the most arduous kind for years, he puts the same whole-heartedness into the worship and service of his new Master with most blessed results.

His biographer reveals the depth of the Sadhu's prayer life in the following extract: "At times the Sadhu will have almost whole days of solitary communion with his Lord and Master. On occasion he has spent the whole night praying. At other times he has to be content with two hours of devotion in the early morning, in England often from five to seven. When he can find time he extends these two hours to three or four hours. Whenever he is compelled by circumstances to omit or unduly curtail his morning meditation he feels a certain restlessness and unhappiness throughout the day.

"He starts the day by reading a chapter of the Bible, at first rapidly, but making a mental note of those verses which seem particularly rich and suggestive. Then he returns to these verses and lingers over them as long as he feels that he is having fruitful thoughts on them. Then he spends about fifteen or more minutes in collecting his thoughts in preparation for prayer. Then, as he puts it, the Holy Spirit Himself teaches him what to pray for, both in regard to himself and in regard to others. For prayer he has no one posture. He prays sitting, kneeling, sometimes walking. As a Sikh he used to prostrate himself in prayer, but now he does not follow this practice.

"He himself finds time for prayer by cutting out many things which others think essential. Before a meeting he insists on several hours of quiet. If he has to speak in the evening he declines invitations to tea or dinner, though when he has no engagements of pressing importance before him he readily accepts such invitations. When asked as to what a man should do when he has such a short time at his disposal that he must choose between his newspaper and his Bible, he said, 'It is his duty to choose the Bible.' He himself rarely reads the papers. He says, in the first place, he has no time, and, in the second place, he is not concerned with politics.

"When once asked how a business man, for example, could find time for prayer when he had to rush his breakfast in order to be at his office in time, the Sadhu pointedly replied, 'Prayer is as important to him as his breakfast. How can he get along without prayer any more than he can without food? If he once begins to form the habit of prayer he will find so much pleasure in it that he will somehow or other find the time for it. . . . Prayer is as important as breathing. We never say, "We have no time to breathe."'"

Amy Carmichael

Many of our readers will have appreciated the books of Amy Carmichael of the Donhavur Fellowship who did a wonderful work in rescuing children from the very claws of Satan himself and of seeing them become mature Christian characters. She encountered great opposition and her conflicts were many. This experienced soldier of the cross can teach us much about the importance of prayer in the missionary's life:

"If prayer matters then it ought not to be counted continually second in our scene of life. . . . All the time the devil is fighting our half-hour's prayer, he never tires of fighting it. Sometimes there is a dullness which is a cloud of hell, sometimes a fiery assault.

"'We know that we have the petitions that we desired of Him.' We pray from the ground of that certainty; not towards certainty, but from it. Is that why we have the words, 'In everything by prayer and supplication with thanksgiving'? We give thanks before we see. Then the thought came, 'What is it that we have in this sense already received? Surely just this: that the glory of the Lord will be manifested (for is not this what we desired of Him?), and that the very best will be done from His eternal point of view, for the work committed to us.'

"Yesterday we had the prayer-meeting in my room, and the one thing we prayed about was prayer. I know we have all, for some time back, felt the need of something more in our prayer-life. I have, personally, and I know others have, and there are many in our Family who come to prayer- meetings because it is the custom to do so, but who are not urged by a great desire. It is the lack of prayer-hunger that often makes a big united meeting difficult. The one thing we seem to need most is a revived prayer-life in our own souls—then the waves will flow out to the others. So we prayed on those lines, and God was with us. I think we shall go on, waiting on Him together for a few minutes every day till we go down (from the Forest). If we prepare the wood, the fire will fall and kindle it. It was wonderful to be in the prayer-meeting after the two long years, and so good to feel the living throb of the other five. The hour passed like five minutes.

"A new desire has been born in me. It is that none of you may miss the peculiar blessing there is in united prayer. Two little sticks burning together can make a glow, thank God; but how much more warm the glow of forty or fifty if each be on fire? The loving, living, present Lord preserve your meetings from ever becoming stale, tepid, ineffective. May they always be as those blessed fifteen minutes were to me, kindling and creative, spirit and life." (From *Amy Carmichael of Donhavur* by Frank Houghton, published by S.P.C.K. Used by permission)

Walker of Tinnevelly

Miss Carmichael also wrote the fascinating story of the labors of a neighboring missionary, "Walker of Tinnevelly," who was a great help and inspiration to her. This is what she has to say about his deep and prevailing prayer life:

"I was thrown with him as a fellow-worker time after time in missions, in conventions, or student camps. I often found myself unable, through sheer lack of physical strength or of spiritual attainment, to hold on with him in the lonely hours of continued and concentrated prayer; or in the terrible soul struggles, as he sought to turn the tide in a convention or meeting from defeat to victory, from indifference to spiritual hunger, and from sin to righteousness, in the vast throngs that he faced from time to time. Truly he was one of God's noblemen, an Elijah of modern times, a John the Baptist, a prophet of righteousness, a watcher in the lonely heights, fearless in conflict, whether he met with the praise or the blame of men. He combined elements of character rare indeed in our superficial and worldly age. His was a life that was holy, humble, and that seemed to keep 'the unstained spirit of a little child.' His was a mind pure as the heart of a flame.

"Every Monday morning was given chiefly to prayer; and the time that supplied the sinews of strength for the day's duty was won by early rising and retiring early at night."

In another place the author describes the place Rev. Walker ascribed to prayer: "There was much prayer throughout the whole time: it was the very breath of life to him: 'Oh, to be able to pray!' he used to say, and then he would pray, and pray, till those who were with him could only wonder that the heavens did not visibly open and pour the blessing down.... Never to him was granted that which, to judge by descriptions in current religious literature, is often granted to some, an open and visible, great ingathering of the precious fruits of the earth. But man after man with whom he came into contact can witness, better still can show a life that witnesses, to what no mortal can effect, or continue to enable if effected. Such were the signs of his apostleship. 'Now go and live for others,' was often his last word to one and another who came, usually alone, to tell him what had happened in the soul's secret place. 'Keep close to God, and go and live for others.' It was his own life practice in two sentences. Spiritual selfishness was, like all insincerity, intolerable to him."

Finally, Miss Carmichael shares a few pungent quotes from this man of prayer: "The secret of failure everywhere is the neglect of private communion with God. India lives too public a life to have a deep Christianity. And Indian Christians will have to alter many of their customs before they get deeper."

And again: "It is better to do a little well and prayerfully than to fulfil a whole world of engagements with undue haste and rush." (Used by permission)

John Hyde

Doubtless few missionaries have given prayer a more prominent place in the their lives than did John Hyde. It is a fact that it was prayer and prayer only that makes Hyde's name worth remembering. He did not just consider prayer important. He counted it *the work*. He literally became a martyr by his life of arduous praying, but oh, the blessed results that followed and the shining example he has set us all who labor abroad or at home! No sacrifice was too great. His biographer, Captain E. G. Carre, writes of him:

"It is this that strikes us so forcibly in Hyde. He challenged God and God challenged him, and he would take hold of God and would not let Him go. God would take hold of him and humble him, and make him almost a laughing-stock at one time, hated at another time, but he just clung to God whatever men might say or do, and with what result! Is not this a challenge to us from the Living God to venture all on Him? 'To let go' is not easy; 'to take the plunge' needs faith; 'to continue' in spite of adverse circumstance—these are marks or signs that the challenge has been accepted. To the timid ones the account of Hyde's life during the next few years that we shall record, viz, 1900 and onwards, will be most encouraging."

The account of a blessed convention where God worked mightily, and the part "Praying" Hyde took in it by praying, should stir us all immensely:

"It was determined that prayer and not preaching should be recognized as the great channel of blessing. To this end a prayer-room was established as the Power House of the movement. Here before the Convention began, Hyde and his friends spent thirty days and thirty nights in prayer, and throughout the ten days of the Convention, Hyde really lived here.

"He spent most of the time on his face, for he felt he never could get low enough before God, pausing sometimes to take a little food and at times throwing himself down in a corner for a little sleep. He shunned publicity, but when he did speak, though his utterance was quiet, his words had a burning power. In the prayer-room he obtained the Tongue of Fire."

The ever-increasing goal which he set himself as regards seeing souls definitely transformed is astounding:

"It was about this time that John Hyde laid hold of God in a very definite covenant. This was for one soul a day, not less, not enquirers simply, but a soul saved, ready to confess Christ in public and be baptized in His Name. Now the stress and strain were relieved. His heart was filled with the peace of full assurance.

"He returned to his district with this confidence, nor was he disappointed. It meant long journeys, nights of watching unto prayer, and fasting, pain, and conflict, yet victory always crowned this. The Good Shepherd was seeing of the travail of His soul and being satisfied. By the end of that year more than 400 souls were gathered in.

"Was he satisfied? Far from it. John Hyde seemed always to be hearing the Good Shepherd's voice saying, 'Other sheep I have. Other sheep I have.' No matter if he won the one a day, he had an unsatisfied longing, an undying passion for lost souls. Love won him victories.

"Two souls a day. Again he laid hold of God with a definite and importunate request. It was for two souls a day. He used to say, 'When we keep near to Jesus, it is He Who draws souls to Himself through us. He must be lifted up in our lives.' God answered his prayers; in that year he had the joy of winning 800 souls to Christ.

"The 800 souls gathered in did not satisfy John Hyde. God was enlarging his heart with His love. Once more he laid hold on God with holy desperation, for four souls a day. In the following year God used him all over India in special meetings and Conferences. God answered his prayers for four souls every day."

But he paid the price! "But the corn of wheat must die. In 1911 he was examined by a doctor, who assured him that unless he ceased from the strain of his intercessory labors he would die within six months. His heart was in an extraordinary state; it had shifted from its natural place on the left to the right side of his body and could only be restored by perfect quiet. But John Hyde now knew why he had been sent into the world. For him life meant prayer. He left the doctor's presence with a radiant face. It had ever been his desire, oft expressed, that he might burn out and not rust out. He would die praying."

Chapter Fourteen

MISSIONARIES IN AFRICA

Africa is much in the news today. With her upheavals and strife, one is apt to overlook the mighty accomplishments of missionaries in that great continent, who have by prayer, devotion, and courage taken the Banner of the Cross from the Cape to Cairo, destroying the slave trade, bringing into the Church of Jesus Christ many thousands of the most genuine Christians to be found anywhere. Exploration, medicine, and education have been invaluable, but it has been the praying missionary, illustrated by the dying Livingstone on his knees, who has wrought the great miracles of grace.

David Livingstone

Livingstone's Journals breathe out prayer after prayer of intense longing and desire. When in the flush of travel and achievement he wrote:

"To Thee, O God, we look. And oh! Thou Who wert the Man of sorrows for the sake of poor vile sinners, and didst not disdain the thief's petition, remember me and Thy cause in Africa. Soul and body, my family and Thy cause, I commit all to Thee. Hear, Lord, for Jesus' sake."

When sick, alone, and facing the most gigantic forces of evil he continued:

"All I can add in my loneliness is, may Heaven's richest blessing come down on every one—American, English, or Turk—who will help to heal the open sore of the world." It happened that the words were written precisely a year before his death.

On the next to his last birthday, he breathed this prayer of dedication:

"My Jesus, my King, my Life, my All; I again dedicate my whole self to Thee. Accept me, and grant, O gracious Father, that ere this year is gone I may finish my task. In Jesus' Name I ask it. Amen. So let it be."

That he vitally depended on prayer is shown clearly in the following:

"When employed in active travel, my mind becomes inactive, and the heart cold and dead, but after remaining some time quiet, the heart revives, and I become more spiritually-minded. This is a mercy which I have experienced before, and when I see a matter to be duty I go on regardless of my feelings. I do trust that the Lord is with me, though the mind is engaged in other matters than the spiritual. I want my whole life to be out and out for the Divine glory, and my earnest prayer is that God may accept what His own Spirit must have implanted—the desire to glorify Him.

"I have been more than usually drawn out in earnest prayer of late—for the expedition—for my family—the fear lest ___'s misrepresentation may injure the cause of Christ—the hope that I may be permitted to open this dark land to the blessed Gospel. I have cast all before my God. Good Lord, have mercy upon me. Leave me not, nor forsake me. He has guided well in time past. I commit my way to Him for the future. All I have received has come from Him. Will He be pleased in mercy to use me for His glory? I have prayed for this, and Jesus Himself said, 'Ask, and ye shall receive,' and a host of statements to the same effect.

"There is a great deal of trifling frivolousness in not trusting in God. Not trusting in Him Who is truth itself, faithfulness, the same yesterday, today and for ever! It is presumption not to trust in Him implicitly and yet this heart is sometimes fearfully guilty of distrust. I am ashamed to think of it. Ay, but He must put the trusting, loving, childlike spirit in by His grace. O Lord, I am Thine, truly I am Thine—take me—do what seemeth good in Thy sight with me, and give me complete resignation to Thy will in all things."

Alexander Mackay

Henry Stanley went to Africa to find Livingstone, which he did, but his visit also had other far-reaching results. Stanley's visit to

King Mtesa of Uganda was the means of challenging another young Scotsman, Alexander Mackay. Faced with insurmountable odds, it was well that Mackay had been born and reared on prayer and knew well the value of it. His engineering skill was the great key to unlock doors but "The White Man of Work" knew only too well that prayer alone would bring Christ into those darkened hearts. In his diary was early recorded this prayer:

"Lord, enable us to search our hearts and humble ourselves before Thee. Oh, for a closer walk with God, more faith, more sincerity, more earnestness, and more love. I must study more the Word of God. 'If ye abide in Me, and My words abide in you, ask whatsoever ye will, and it shall be done unto you.' The Master said so, and His words are true."

The great secret behind Mackay, however, was a praying mother. We quote from his biographer: "Daily, almost hourly, her prayers ascended for his welfare. Her great hope was that his life should be dedicated to the Master's cause, the sacredness of which had been increased by the stainless life and the holy devotion of her husband. This hope she was never privileged to see fulfilled.

"Her last days and nights were spent in prayer for her boy, and when the end was approaching more rapidly than the messenger could bring Alexander to her, she handed a godly attendant her most precious souvenir, to be given to him when the last scene was over. It was her Bagster's Bible which had been presented to her as a wedding gift by her husband. To her it had been one of the dearest of mute companions, and she gave instructions that certain passages, specially applicable to the needs of her son, should be prominently marked, in the hope that they would flash conviction across his mind.

"Her repeated prayers were abundantly answered; and if Christians can behold after death the things of time and sense (as some authorities aver), she would be more than abundantly satisfied with the nobility of purpose which was created within her son's breast by her last prayerful injunction, 'Search the Scriptures.'"

Dan Crawford

There is no doubt but that the effective missionary has always given prayer and the Word a fundamental place in his or her life. The missionary life is an extremely busy one, but the men and women who have kept power in spite of surrounding degradation, those whose lives have been filled with love and resultant blessing, have placed prayer and Bible Study above every requisite.

We can only touch here and there on the prayer emphasis of the numberless praying missionaries to the Dark Continent. Take for example, Dan Crawford:

"Above all, Dan gave himself to Bible Study and prayer. The habit of regular, quiet worship, shutting the door to exclude external hindrances, to be alone with God and thus to ponder His Word and allow it to speak to the heart; and then pouring out the soul in adoration, intercession, and supplication, is the chief thing in the culture of the devout life."

Samuel Zwemer

In no field of labor would one feel more dependent on God than in work among the Muslims. Oh, the many missionaries who have worked and prayed their hearts out for God to break in that rocky soil! We have personally known some of the contemporary laborers and our hearts yearn in prayer that they may see results.

An example of these praying missionaries to the Muslims was Samuel Zwemer, missionary and editor.

"The history of missions," said Dr. S. M. Zwemer, "is the history of answered prayer. . . it is the key to the whole missionary problem. All human means are secondary. The work of missions from start to finish is a miracle of God's grace. So stupendous is the task, so great the obstacles and opposition that 'if we in our own strength confide, our striving would be losing.' We must invoke and rely upon supernatural power."

We need not wonder that Zwemer cultivated prayer in his own life. In the book, *Apostle to Islam*, J. Christy Wilson comments:

"His diary shows that the regular habits of personal devotions and prayer had been established, which were his abiding source of power. He writes, 'George Müller's life of trust makes one feel the power of prayer. Why can we not all live that way?'

"We find that he continued the hour of prayer and Bible reading from noon to one o'clock, which had been established the first year in Seminary. Before a major address for the Student Volunteer Movement, he records, 'Felt very weak spiritually but prayer was strengthening.' Again and again he noted that he was greatly helped in speaking, as an answer to prayer."

"Unless we take time to be holy, there will be no holiness for us in eternity," wrote Zwemer. "Some things cannot be done in a hurry. True prayer takes time. There are processes of growth and development in nature that can by no artificial means be hastened. The tree 'that looks to God all day and lifts her leafy arms to pray' is not the mushroom growth of a summer night. We need time before we pray to realize God's presence, while we are praying to realize our own and the world's need, and after we have prayed to meditate on God's wonderful grace and to thank Him for what He has promised.

"Every element in the missionary problem today depends for its solution chiefly upon prayer. The present-day summons to the Church, as Dr. John R. Mott points out, is to tap the supernatural resources of God Almighty by believing prayer. He can control the hearts of men. He can release the energies of His Church. He can overcome man's selfishness and greed. Prayer will thrust out laborers and provide for their support."

Lilias Trotter

Lilias Trotter, founder of the Algiers Mission Band, realized the importance of intercessory prayer on behalf of her difficult work among the Muslims:

"He has begun to show me how He has called us to share the life of Jesus in intercession, how men are to be reached by prayer in the Holy Ghost—prayer which fights through and prevails; how then, and only then, can the windows of Heaven open on the barren land? . . . What we want is to have our faith brought down to the uttermost simplicity, to the absolute transparent childlikeness of those words, 'I believe in God.' It can be so when, as someone said the other day, there is nothing between our bare hearts and Jesus."

In her book, *The Master of the Impossible,* this intrepid adventurer said: "The promise that has been alive these days is Matthew 18:18, 'Whatsoever ye shall bind on earth shall be bound in heaven, and whatsoever ye shall loose on earth shall be loosed in heaven.' It is framed in on either side by the condition of unity of spirit. And this 'binding' and 'loosing' seems to be the true sphere of prayer. The two parables of intercession help mark this out as a battlefield of prayer— the friend on the midnight errand loosing the powers of life; the widow in her importunity binding the power of death."

Rowland Bingham

The key to the success of a great mission to Africa, The Sudan Interior Mission, can be summed up in the words of the founder, Rowland Bingham, who wrote: "It was the impassioned pleading of a little Scotch lady that linked up my life with the Sudan."

That little woman was Mrs. Gowans who so carried the Sudan on her heart in prayer that she gladly gave her son, Walter Gowans, to be a corn of wheat, disappearing in burial under Nigerian soil, after only a brief time in that Continent.

"With her prayer and faith she carried us from the first seven, barren years into the years of harvest," said Rowland Bingham.

When her son fell a victim to malaria in a small village, that mother prayed that God would raise up a witness on that spot where her son yielded up his last breath. A party of six missionaries later chose that same village for a mission center not, knowing the prayer request of that interceding mother. "They were held in that place by Mrs. Gowans' prayers," said the founder when viewing the harvest yield in later years.

A few statements from this daring pioneer will reveal the estimate he placed upon prayer:

"The danger of our day is devotion to duty to the neglect of personal communion. We will do far more and far better if we carefully guard against hindering our times of communion with Him.

"As well try to draw water out of a dry well as to try to carry on

Christian service without drawing present life from the Living Vine.

"Christian, beware! Declension is always a slow leak, never a blowout. Flatness in spiritual living and serving is the result of a gradual slipping away from God in prayer and Bible Study, a neglecting of the means of grace."

J. H. Hunter, who wrote Bingham's biography, said: "Rowland Bingham was a man of one Book. Someone has said that such a man is to be feared. If that be true, then the subject of this work was one to be dreaded. This does not mean he was not familiar with other works that men have written. He was. But one Book dominated his life and thought. It shaped his plans and purposes. From its sacred depths he drew strength, sustenance, wisdom, and refreshment. He believed it implicitly, that it meant what it said, and would be a lamp to the feet and a light to the path of all who put their trust therein. It was to him the living Word of the Living God, a God-inspired volume that contained the only answer to the deepest problems of life and which alone could shed a light on human destiny."

And because of this, he was a man of prayer and faith and searchingly commended prayer to his comrades. He writes:

"'He wondered that there was no intercessor.'

"'He marveled because of their unbelief.'

"Two things that cause God to wonder now will be our greatest marvel by and by: 1. That we did not pray more. 2. That we did not trust more. He marvels now—we shall marvel when we see Him. The most marvelous thing of today is the unbelief of the Christians."

Johanna Veenstra

Eva Stuart Watt has written a most thrilling story of Johanna Veenstra, a lady missionary to cannibals in Nigeria who over and over again stresses the utter dependence on prayer. At the beginning, she describes a praying band of missionaries consecrating their lives and being filled by the Holy Spirit. Oh, if such conferences were in evidence now!

"Hours alone with God, with no one to see or hear but the Lord, were customary; but the fellowship of others in prayer or praise *for hours,* could it be downright real? On entering the room, the problem was solved. At once you knew only reality. Others in the room were forgotten, except when the combined prayers and praises made you realize the strength and power and sympathy of such fellowship. Communion with others were precious times, when together we waited on God to search us and to speak to us, together interceded for souls, together praised Him for Himself and for His wonder-working power.

"There was a breadth and freedom during those ten days that I never imagined existed on earth. Surely it was for freedom such as this that Christ had set us free. Each one did exactly as he or she felt led to do. Some went to bed early; some prayed for hours; some prayed all night long. Some went to the meetings and some to the prayer-room. Some prayed, some praised; some sat to pray, some kneeled, some lay prostrate on their faces before God, just as the Holy Spirit led them. There was no criticism, no judging of what was being done or said. Everyone realized that superficialities were put away and that each was in the awful presence of a Holy God."

"I'm convinced," wrote Jennie Stielstra, her co-worker, "that the inner closet was the secret of her success as a missionary." She said, herself, to another colleague one day, "Never an hour passes but I am conscious of the immediate presence of God." So here was a missionary "broken in" by the Lord.

Later we get another picture of this praying missionary—this time of nightly prayer vigils:

"While the wild night breeze was still blowing from the hills, Johanna would be up alone with God, her Bible open before a hurricane lamp on a camp table. It was there she saw God's face and heard His voice, there she found daily manna for her soul, there she had fanned the fires of love that burned out all day long for souls."

Prayer sessions together brought signal victories:

"They fought on their knees, bombarding the devil's trenches with the never-failing promises of God. The Lord of the battle, they knew, delighted in Impossibilities. So by faith they reached up to the Throne and brought down reinforcements: 'out of weakness were made strong, waxed valiant in fight.' Their pleading was no crackling of thorns, but a divine fire that burnt their own hearts while it blazed for souls. They prayed till they had the assurance that God had heard them and they were through to victory. No wonder they went to bed very often with a big Hallelujah inside, and fresher many a time than when they started in the morning!"

Faced with witchcraft and battling for a soul, prayer was her only weapon all through that night.

We sometimes hear that missionaries feel they must not offend the natives, but must always be at their beck and call. This was not so with Johanna and her fellow-missionary: "We would take it in turn to shut ourselves in there with God," she wrote. "The natives knew they were not to disturb us, and they never broke their trust."

She recounts, too, a wonderful answer to prayer experienced by the Africans. Surely the people among whom we work become like us!

Time would fail us to recount all the prayer-experiences of just one missionary. May all workers for God at home and abroad make prayer their first and last line of defence and their essential weapon of attack.

Brethren, let us pray!

Chapter Fifteen

UNTIL SIN WAS UNCOVERED

The following was a true incident taken from a sermon preached by Rev. H. Robb French in 1964. We include this in our revival chapters because we feel that today there are many similar circumstances existing in the religious world. The Church is throttled; members are leaving, and no one is praying things through. Those knowing the hindrances are unwilling to divulge any incidents relevant to the situation and God's Spirit leaves the Church until such a time as some brave servant of the Lord rises up and faces the situation through prayer.

Nina was just such a person. This then is her story:

"One reason why it is so hard to have a revival is that there is so much to think about; so many luxuries; so many things to appreciate. Israel needed a revival, and we need one; we surely do. Here is the beginning: 'Until that I, a mother in Israel, arose.' Do you get the full purport of those words? 'I, a mother in Israel.' Who is a mother? She's the one that travails and brings forth lives.

"An announcement came out in the *Wesleyan* announcing the death of a certain lady. I read it over and haven't forgotten it but somehow or other I seldom mention it. As I read over the announcement of the death of this lady who was killed in an automobile wreck, I lived over those days. We were in Camp-Meeting and she was in the school there. A group of girls joined hands with her and took a vow that they would pray until a revival came. Those of us who attended would be sitting eating dinner in the dining hall and we would hear them up in the Dormitory or maybe in the Administration Building praying. They usually prayed in subdued tones. We would wake up in the night and hear them praying. They weren't praying loud; they were praying in subdued tones, but we knew they were praying. It wasn't easy to eat; it wasn't too easy to sleep, though they were very considerate about people having their sleep.

"And here's what they said, 'We have had great camp-meetings on these grounds, but we feel we have got to have something greater than we have ever had before. And we feel it is up to us to pray through on the matter.'

"I got up to preach one afternoon and Nina came up on the platform and asked, 'Could I say a few words, Brother French?' She was very reticent and not forward at all. It wasn't like her, but I knew the Spirit of God was resting on her, so I said, 'Certainly, Nina.'

"She said, 'I feel that it's going to take my life. We must have a greater camp-meeting than we have ever had before. And a group of us feel that way and we are praying about it. I have bid my parents good-bye. I have bid my sister in Africa good-bye, because I feel it's going to take my life. I have given it to the Lord, and if it takes my life it's alright.' There wasn't any note of pride or selfishness about it, just such a humble spirit about her. You would have to know her to appreciate her. She spoke just those few words, and then she went down and knelt at the altar. She sank down in genuine soul travail. Nina groaned like she was dying.

"Well, the crowd gathered that night, but somehow or other it seemed impossible to have a service. She was there praying and it looked like she was dying. So I said, 'Well, if we're not going to have preaching, let's gather round and pray.' We gathered around and prayed. Many left. It was mostly preachers and preachers' wives who remained in the tabernacle. Nina kept on groaning. The service took on the form of a confession meeting. The preachers would get up and confess, 'I haven't had a revival in my charge this year.' 'I feel like I haven't prayed; I haven't had a burden.' 'I feel like I'm to blame.'

"Preachers' wives would get up and confess. One preacher rose and said, 'I haven't been as kind in my home as I ought to. I have been cross and irritable with my wife. I want to ask her to forgive me. I want the church to forgive me.' But he remained as cold as a cucumber and sat down.

"We prayed on and people would shout, but Nina didn't come up. An old friend of ours, a preacher in the conference, said, 'Now friends, when we get at the hindering cause, she's coming up from here. Maybe we're shouting too quick. Let's hold on here till we get through.' We went down again and confession broke out anew. Finally she seemed to come back to consciousness somewhat and shook her head and said, 'We haven't struck it yet.' I don't know whether she knew who she was burdened for or not. I don't think she did. But she knew she was bringing forth a Camp-Meeting.

"I guess it was long after 12 midnight when a young girl slipped out of the tabernacle and called some ladies out. I don't like to tell these details at all, but maybe I'd better just mention them briefly and carefully. Well, she called some ladies out and she said, 'Now that lady is going to die. She can't stand that much longer. She's getting weak. I can bring her up from there, and I'll be responsible if I don't. If you'll call a certain preacher out here, I'll face him, and she'll come up from there.'

"Now the preacher was the one who had gotten up and said he hadn't been as kind as he should. I think he made three confessions. Mrs. French told me about his sin, and I went and knelt down where this brother was kneeling, and I said, 'Brother, this burden is for you.'

"'Oh no, Brother French, it couldn't be that.'

"'But,' I said, 'it is!'

"'Oh no, I'm saved and sanctified. I've got the victory, Brother French; God has been blessing me.'

"'But the burden is for you, sir.'

"'No, Mr. French, you're wrong.'

"I said, 'Sir, your sin is out. You might as well confess it. The only hope for you is to go to the bottom. You'll gain nothing by denying it.'

"So he knelt a little while. He was a sixty-year-old man and he had ruined a sixteen-year-old girl. He said, 'Pray for me, Brother French, that I'll feel the guilt of my sin.'

"I've never gotten over the shock of that. A sixty-year-old man, he was staying in a home where he was pasturing a church, and he ruined that father's youngest girl, and yet here he was saying, 'Pray that I'll feel the guilt of my sin; I don't feel it.' Well, he didn't confess what he had done but got up and said that he had sinned. It was no place to confess what he had done but he said, 'I have sinned, I've been a hypocrite.'

"Nina came up from there looking like an angel. I thought maybe she was going to Heaven right from there because her face glowed. And do you know what happened in that conference? That conference had been dying, slowly dying, year after year, losing members. But when that sin was cleared up it began to grow by leaps and bounds. The revival spirit began to sweep through that conference and they told me, 'Why they're calling for us, Brother French, "Come over here, organize us in a church."' How do you account for it? A mother in Israel. Charles Finney said, 'I have never seen them sweat blood like Jesus did in the garden, but I have seen their noses bleed.'

"Brother, a burden like that is what we need. It's out of date! It's in reproach! It wouldn't be tolerated in a lot of places, but I'd like to see some fathers and mothers in Israel grace the Church again who'll go down into the jaws of death to pick up an old sinner down there who'll never get saved unless he's carried—like that man out there with the palsy, unless somebody carries him he's lost. We can't carry them physically, but we can carry them on our hearts, and we can carry them to Jesus. I'd like to know more about that. The flesh shrinks from it, but oh, I believe it's the greatest ministry that God ever committed to poor mortal people—when His Spirit comes upon the saints, till they bring forth revival.

"'Until I, a mother in Israel, arose.' 'The people willingly offered themselves.' Don't you like that? That thrills me! Israel has a challenge; she's fighting for her liberty, fighting for her life and the people. What is that? That is the language of consecration. A sister and I were saying the other day that people discard the word consecration as though it doesn't mean much, but that's because they don't know their Bibles. Joseph Smith said, 'Crucifixion and consecration are synonymous.' They are! When you consecrate, you are crucified; you are abandoned; you are no longer your own. It's a covenant, a covenant with God." (Used by permission).

Chapter Sixteen

REVIVAL IN THE CONGO

An account of a revival scene in the Congo which appeared in *Worldwide Magazine* is most interesting and touching. Charlie Searle had been an eye-witness, and the article is a stenographic report of his speech.

What a shock it was when news of the Belgian Government's edict reached us! It looked as though we would not only have to close some of our existing stations but also be unable to reach the totally unevangelized areas that were so heavy on our hearts. Twelve stations manned by whites was to be the limit permitted to any mission society, and we were already over that quota.

After much prayer and consideration, the mission decided to move workers from two stations. One was in the Mubudu tribe at Imbai, where Jack Roberts and his two sisters, Lily and Ivy were working, and one in the Malika tribe, for which my wife and I were responsible.

Jack Roberts was asked to pioneer in a new area, five days march through dense forest, while his sisters were to stay six months at Imbai to make final preparations for leaving. Faced with the tremendous responsibility of preparing the native Christians to be left alone, the sisters decided to cancel all station activity and spend the time waiting upon God for guidance. Sometimes they prayed together, while at other times they met the Lord separately; but they spent the whole of the three days with Him.

At the end of this time, Lily said to her younger sister, "I feel that God has spoken to me. I prayed, 'Lord, if Thou wouldst only send a revival, a second Pentecost, we would not need to fear that these babes in Christ would go back into heathenism. They would be established in Thee.' To this He replied, 'You have asked a hard thing; nevertheless, if you can pay the price, you may have what you asked.'" Her response was, "Lord, my life for Revival!"

Then God began to prepare them for the blessing He was going to send. He showed them many things in their lives that were not pleasing to Him: criticism, impatience, careless gossip, and unkind things they had said and thought about people. He had them write letters of confession, humbling letters, asking forgiveness for thought or word that was not worthy of the Lord. Remember, these were devoted, consecrated women, but they were seeking a mighty outpouring of God's Spirit. They started regular meetings with those Christians who were prepared to go all the way with God, and to walk in all the light that He would give. Those who were not willing to accept these conditions in waiting upon God for the outpouring of His Spirit, were asked to stay away.

It was usual for the sisters to rise at five-thirty each morning to meet the Lord; but as time went on and the burden increased, He got them up earlier and earlier until they were rising at two forty-five. They would read the Word and pray together and then separately and individually wait upon God until six-thirty. At that time they would meet with the Christians and share what had been revealed to them through the Word earlier.

One morning it was laid on Lily's heart to give up their schools and to spend all of the time in prayer. (One was in charge of the girls' school, and the other the boys'.) However, she did not feel that they could send the children back to their heathen homes and the sinful influences there. But just at that time the two assistant principals came and said that God had spoken to each individually but with the same word, that they should take full responsibility for the schools and release the sisters to pray.

Now I must mention how I came into contact with all this: Our station was only 26 miles from Imbai, and my wife and I were very close friends of the Roberts. As we were the nearest workers to the post office, all mail for the area was cleared through us. I first noticed that something unusual was happening at Imbai when the mail began to dwindle until just once in every two weeks a letter went to their mother, that was all.

One day a runner came from Imbai for the mail, and I greeted him with the question, "What is the news, Batabombi?"

He looked at me rather peculiarly, I thought, and replied, "Bwana, it is the news of prayer."

"News of prayer? What is that?"

"I mean we pray in a new way at our station."

I said, "What do you mean? I don't understand you."

"Well, Bwana, if you visited our station when the sun was beginning to rise, you would see all the people outside their huts, reading the Word of God and praying. When the sun comes there (pointing to 6:30), the drum sounds and the people pour into the church. And there they remain until the sun is there (noon), or there (six p.m.), or there (midnight)."

"What! You stay all day in the church praying, and sometimes until midnight?"

"That is so."

"Oh," I thought, "this man is dreaming. He is talking through the back of his head. It can't be true. We would have heard something about it."

I spoke to other missionaries on the station and they said, "Just native exaggeration." So, although we thought about it, we said very little. A few days later the rumor came from a different source; so, when I was at our head station, I mentioned it. It was suggested that, as it was only ten miles farther around, I should call in at Imbai on my way home. A fellow missionary, Herman Meyer, from America, offered to drive me in his car; so we decided to make the visit.

When we arrived at Imbai, we made our way to the house and began firing questions. They smiled a little wearily, I thought, and said, "We will try to tell you what we can." Very quietly Lily told us of God's dealings with them and with the natives in much more detail than I have given. The Lord appeared unto her in a vision, she told us. It seemed as though Heaven opened, and she saw Him, looking down at her. Opposite her was the wife of the Leading Christian in the village, but between them was a barrier. Pointing to the native woman, the Lord said, "This woman is as precious to Me as you are. She is redeemed and cleansed by My Blood, the same as you. But you look upon her as just a native woman, while you are a white lady. This is hidden pride, which I have not been able to show you until now. This stands between you and Revival."

When speaking of this, Lily was absolutely overawed; and her voice dropped to a whisper. The Lord's rebuke had smitten her down, and she wept for hours before Him. Then He came and touched her and brought peace to her heart. With it came such a consciousness of His presence that as she walked from room to room, she felt that He was literally walking by her side.

Each Wednesday, the Christians from the area round about came to the station to join in seeking the Lord. The day of the vision was Wednesday, and she didn't know how to face the Christians when they came for the meeting. When it was time to start, she went to the platform without looking at the people. She announced no hymn, she prayed no prayer; but she confessed to them the hidden pride which the Lord had shown her: how she had felt that she was better than they, even though they were souls for whom Jesus had died. In the group of perhaps one hundred before her, were men who had been cannibals, and women who had been the Jezebels of heathendom before their conversion. But as she looked down, she saw that they were all melted to tears.

Then things began to happen! One man stood up and confessed to robbing another man's trap ten years before. He said that he was going to confess to the man and pay for the gazelle he had stolen. People began confessing all kinds of sins, from the grosser ones—to criticism, lack of reading the Word and prayer, coldness, hard thoughts, and gossip. They went to one another to ask forgiveness and to put things right. Finally they became just like one person, cemented together by absolute love—nothing between. As on the day of Pentecost, "They were all with one accord" (Acts. 2:1). Two days later the Spirit came down upon these people in a mighty Baptism. That is why the man said to me, "We pray in a new way on our station."

A great burden of prayer came upon them also, so that sometimes after praying all day, they would go out into the forest and pray all night. If you could hear the roaring of the leopards and the howling of the hyenas and jackals in the forest, you would not be too keen to spend the night there. But when the Power of God came upon these people, fear fled to the wind!

When her story was finished, Lily asked, "With the permission of you gentlemen I would like to invite some of the natives to join us in prayer. Do you mind?" (This was one time in the day when whites and blacks had their prayer-meetings separate.) Of course we did not mind. Turning to one of her boys, she said, "Go down to the village and tell Lapuno to invite twenty or twenty-five—not more than twenty-five—to join us in prayer here. Mind, not more than that."

I haven't usually found people falling over themselves to get to prayer-meeting. You seldom have to lock the door to keep them out. But, here they had to keep it quiet as the room would be crowded with twenty-five. That prayer-meeting will always live in my memory. I had never heard praying quite like that before. It seemed as if a mighty rushing wind had come into our midst. I was mystified, trying to understand, "What is it? What is it?" I felt as if my Christian experience had suddenly become nothing, and my heart had turned to stone. I was in the midst of people who were in the presence of God!

Herman managed to stop the prayer-meeting at midnight. I don't think I would ever have been able to stop it. The people with beaming faces shook our hands and left. I was very quiet and sober, almost in a dream. Lily turned to me and said, "We are starting evangelistic meetings tomorrow morning at nine o'clock. When I saw you get out of the car, I thanked the Lord for sending the first speaker."

"Oh excuse me," I said, "I must get back to my station. I will have to get away early. I must get back." I thought, "I am not going to try to preach to these folk. They should be preaching to me."

She replied, "I am very disappointed. You see, we are very tired. We felt that God had been so gracious in sending someone to help us."

I felt so mean that I consented to stay. In the morning there was a knock at the door and a voice said, "The food is ready and the hour is past." I looked at my watch; it was eight-thirty. (Breakfast was at eight and the meeting at nine.) So, I picked up my Bible and went into the house. Just Ivy was there, so I asked, "Where is Lily?"

"Oh, she has been in the meeting for three hours with the natives. They are having a prayer-meeting," she replied.

At five to nine I went into the church, and there was Lily kneeling on the mud floor, translating out of the English Bible some of the promises she had received early that morning. She had been up as usual at 2:45 praying. Now at nine in the morning, the drum was beating, and the people were pouring into the church until it was crowded with over a thousand. It was a huge place. We sang a few hymns. Then I began to preach. When I had finished I started to sit down. But Lily said, "Don't sit down. Make an appeal."

I looked at her in amazement. "Make an appeal after a message like that!"

I walked to the edge of the platform and began to make an appeal; but before I was through, a man sprang to his feet. His face was set, his eyes closed; and he just flung his hands up and cried, "I must get right with God today!"

The effect was electric. All over the church people stood up, not one here and there, but in groups—literally in groups. There were hundreds of people standing, with tears flowing down their faces, not only men and women but also boys and girls. They all wanted to get right with God! I stood there not knowing what to do. "What has happened! What has happened!"

Then God spoke to me: "Not by might, nor by power, but by my Spirit, saith the Lord of Hosts" (Zech. 4:6). He showed me that this was not the result of my poor preaching, but that the price of this harvest had been paid before I arrived. From that day until they had to leave the station, those two missionaries spent all of their time leading souls to the Savior and building them up in the Word. They didn't need to preach.

The Christians went everywhere in that area testifying to the mighty power of God; and every road led to Imbai! Not only the unsaved came, but the backsliders who had grown cold and no longer had any desire for the things of the Lord.

Cost of Revival in Belgian Congo:

Lily Roberts said, "Lord, my life for Revival." That is what happened. It cost her her life. A little later, Lily went to her reward, and I know this, my dear friends, there was an abundant entrance into the Presence of God. (Used by Permission)

"What will it cost?" the people asked
    As they planned the fall campaign;
While in past exploits they calmly basked,
    Looking only for outside gain.

"Three hundred at least for evangelists;
    Twenty for heat and light.
And remember the music enthusiasts."
    What a price for such a small fight.

"What will it cost?" List to Spirit's pleas:
    Praying, fasting, and tears.
Each member humbled on bended knees,
    Confessing the faults of years.

"The rough made smooth, the crooked straight;
    Recourse to repentance's fruit.
The Breath of God on all who wait;
    Healing for blind, deaf, and mute."

If revival comes we will have to pay
    In heavenly currency.
Not a part or e'en half, but ALL we must lay
    At His feet! Is it YOUR plea?
                      —Floyd Banker.
Used by permission as published in the *Wesleyan Methodist*.

BOOKS ON PRAYER BY E. F. & L. HARVEY

Kneeling We Triumph, Books 1 & 2
Each book contains 60 stimulating readings composed of gleanings from the writings of godly men and women.

Royal Exchange.
31 Daily readings on prayer.

How They Prayed, Volumes 1, 2, & 3.
Volume 1 deals with the subject of household prayer, citing many instances of striking answers that have been received.
Volume 2 reveals how godly ministers of the past have had to spend many hours in prayer in order to see lasting results.
Volume 3 shows how missionaries who have done exploits for God and successfully invaded the kingdom of darkness have prayed hard and long. The book also records the mighty praying that has accompanied past revivals.

Asking Father
A book intended for children but which makes excellent reading for adults also. These short, factual stories show the wonderful interest and concern of our Heavenly Father Who delights to hear and answer the prayers of His children.